St. Paul and the Cities

Joe O. Lewis

Dedicated to the faithful Wednesday Night (and Noonday) folks at Mountain Brook Baptist Church, Birmingham, Alabama for whom these presentations were originally prepared.

Contents

Preface

In some ways Paul and Jesus were much alike. After all, Paul could write "For me to live is Christ!" But in some ways they were vastly different. One obvious difference between the Savior and the Saint was their geographical range. Jesus moved mostly between Galilee and Jerusalem with a few excursions away from the line between those two parts of ancient Israel. Paul operated on either side of a line that ran from Antioch in Syria to Rome and he walked most of that line three times-- perhaps travelling as much as 10,000 miles. There are other differences between these two but the one that is at the heart of this book stems from the places on those lines they walked where they stopped. As far as most of us can tell, Jesus stopped only in villages whereas there is not a single instance on all those journeys of Paul in which the great Apostle visited a village, a small town. It may be that archaeologists can make a case for Jesus visiting the large city of Sepphoris just a few miles from Nazareth--indeed it may be quite likely that he did, but none of the Gospel writers ever recorded such a visit. Jesus was born in a village and spent all his life in the villages of Galilee and Judea. Paul was born in a city--Tarsus in Cilicia--and spent all his working life in the cities of the Roman Empire. He must have travelled through hundreds of villages as he walked, but Luke has not noted any of them.

Paul was a city boy. This book tries to set Paul's ministry in the context of the cities he touched in his travels. A few of the cities Luke mentions are not covered--apologies to Beroea in Macedonia and the cities of Cyprus--but most are. The reader needs to be aware, however, that these studies are not technical, scholarly descriptions of the cities Paul visited. The chapters in this book contain studies that were presented on Wednesday nights after supper in a Baptist church. The author is sharing second hand information about cities that, for the most part, he has never visited. There is no new information here, but hopefully putting the cities up front will help make the stories in Acts and in Paul's letters come alive. Those who are familiar with the literature on Paul's journeys will recognize the similarity between the title of this book--*St. Paul and the Cities*--and another book title, *The Cities of St. Paul* by Sir William M. Ramsay. Originally published in 1907, my introduction to the book came when it was reprinted in the 1960 edition during my seminary days. Since then it and the companion volume, *St. Paul the traveller and the Roman Citizen (1897)*, have taught me most of what I know about the subject. Several footnotes in this volume will testify to my dependence but they do not begin to document all the basic knowledge about Roman cities that I've gained from him.

Some readers may be aware that in the last fifty years or so there has been a wealth of attention paid to early urban Christians in an effort to understand who they were and what place they held in the social structure of the first century. These studies are fascinating and provide many ways to flesh out the names we read in many of Paul's postscripts but this book does not attempt to interact with these studies for the most part although a few are cited in the footnotes. Likewise little attempt is made here to deal with archaeological excavations of the cities covered. Some cities such as Ephesus have been explored by generations of scholars but for the most part the information from these excavations is too detailed to cover in these after dinner papers.

Finally, there seems to be an obvious omission from the cities covered. Jerusalem is not there. It is true that the final phase of Paul's life began in Jerusalem when he was arrested there and imprisoned in Caesarea. It is also true that his early adult years apparently were spent studying in Jerusalem. But having said this, Jerusalem does not play a major role in Paul's travels. Opposition to Paul's ministry emerged early in the Jerusalem church and some from Jerusalem (either Jews or Christian Jews) apparently followed Paul into the communities of Antioch, Iconium, Lystra, and Derbe in an effort to undo what he had done in those cities. But Paul did not take his Gospel to Jerusalem as he did to the cities of the Roman world. He took an offering to Jerusalem, but Jerusalem did not contribute to his support as the Philippians did. So I have not included Jerusalem in the cities dealt with here.

As is often the case, studying the Bible allows a person to see something missed in all those previous readings. You will,

I'm confident, find that to be the case as you walk with Paul from city to city in these pages. In some cases, however, studying the Bible makes one painfully aware of what is not said in the text. Time and again in these pages that has been the case for me. I was struck, for example, by the absence of any personal references to Paul's family. When he went back to Tarsus as a Christian I wonder how he was received? Were his parents still alive? Likewise I wonder how the Christians in Rome felt about Paul's letter that we call Romans. Christians met Paul as he approached the city of Rome? Were they in awe of this towering intellect? Did they know about the letter/book? Apparently the Jewish delegation that came to visit him in prison had never heard of Paul's letter or anything else about him. And then there are a host of commonplace things that are never spoken about either by Luke or by Paul. Were there no scenic overlooks anywhere in the mountains he traversed? How did he carry his tent making tools? How heavy were they? Did he have a donkey to help him with his luggage? How much did it cost to take the ship from Troas across the Aegean Sea on his way to Philippi?

Perhaps you may know the answers to these or the thousand other questions that enquiring minds want to know. And as you discuss these chapters--perhaps after supper in a Baptist church somewhere--ask not just what is there but what is not there and why was it not included.

Chapter 1

The Roman World and the Fullness of Time

Let's start with a quiz. Was the Roman Empire friend or foe of the Christian faith? Most of us would answer that the Roman Empire was an enemy of the faith! Upon hearing the question we would probably think immediately of the book of Revelation and "666," the number of the "beast." And, of course, at the moment in time that John wrote his Revelation, Rome most certainly was an enemy even unto death for many Christians. The word "martyr" became the common Christian word for "witness" because so many Christians gave their ultimate testimony by yielding their bodies to terrible tortures and death at the hands of Roman persecutors. There is no doubt then that at some times and in some places during the first three hundred years of church history the Roman Empire and all its might was arrayed against the Christian faith.

If we had the ability to interview common people in Israel during the first century they would testify that anyone who had friends like the Romans really did not need enemies. Farmers in Israel and throughout the Roman world saw much of the food they raised taken by Roman procurators as taxes. Soldiers of every country overrun by the Roman army would testify that

Rome showed no mercy in battle and sometimes took no prisoners.[1] Indigenous peoples everywhere were reduced to the status of slaves when Rome took over—it has been said that more than twenty-five percent of the people of the Roman Empire were slaves in the first century. Shortly after Jesus' lifetime, hatred for the Romans reached a boiling point and Zealots led a revolt against Rome that ended with the destruction of the Temple in Jerusalem and terrible reprisals against the people of towns like Sepphoris which was just three miles from Nazareth. So it would be no surprise if the first Christians looked upon Rome as their enemy.

But, on the other hand, a case might well be made that without the Roman Empire Christianity would have had a much more difficult—if not impossible—task of spreading around the Mediterranean world so quickly. As we begin our look at the cities of the Roman Empire in which the Apostle Paul lived and moved and had his being, we'll look at the Roman world which the Empire made possible. First we'll look at the map and take just a few moments to familiarize ourselves with the territory covered by the Roman Empire in the first century. Then we'll explore four aspects of the Roman world that played a tremendous role in the development of the Christian faith. The subject is vast and, obviously, what we do here will be very superficial.

---

[1] "The victorious legions, who, in distant wars, acquired the vices of strangers and mercenaries, first oppressed the freedom of the republic, and afterwards violated the majesty of the purple." Edward Gibbon, "The Decline and Fall of the Roman Empire," http://www.ccel.org/g/gibbon/decline/volume1/chap39.htm.

But even so we will be reminded that Rome was friend as well as foe to Christians. It was no understatement when Paul wrote to the Galatians (4:4) that "when the fullness of time was come, God sent forth his Son.... ." When the Roman Empire was at its zenith, God found the time ripe for his greatest act. Luke reminded us that it was during the reign of a Roman Emperor, Caesar Augustus, that the fullness of time arrived. And the events that were heralded on Christmas eve that year took place, according to Luke, in a Roman province ruled by a Roman Governor while a Roman census was being taken across the empire.

The Land That Was Roman

A look at the map shows something of the size of the Roman Empire. Already in the time of Jesus, the Empire stretched 2500 miles "as the crow flies" from Spain to Israel. (It is right at 2500 air miles from the Pacific coast to the Atlantic coast!) Paul hoped to go to Spain, but we don't know if he got to make that journey. Paul's Roman world extended from Jerusalem to Rome, some 1500 air miles and at least twice that far over land. Later the Empire would reach further in both directions. From north to south the Empire stretched across the Mediterranean some 800 miles. It took in France and Spain, Austria, Italy, Macedonia, Greece, Turkey, Syria, Lebanon, Egypt, North Africa and more. Of course, what this really means is that armies from Rome had fought their way more than a thousand miles in both directions from Rome itself and had been victorious. Much of what Rome came to rule had been Persian and

Greek before it became Roman, and these great empires left their marks on the peoples and the land as we shall see.

The tiny country of Israel marked the eastern boundary of the Roman Empire in Jesus' lifetime. Soldiers, governors and tax collectors became the everyday face of the Roman Empire to the people of Israel. It was a hundred years after Jesus' crucifixion before a Roman Emperor set foot in Israel; in 130 A.D. Hadrian came to Jerusalem and ultimately precipitated the last Jewish war against Rome with his plans to rebuild Jerusalem as a Roman city.

We Americans are accustomed to our cities looking much the same because of the pervasive franchising that has blurred the local flavor of our regions. It was not so in the Roman Empire. It is not hard to imagine the difference in cities that reached from Damascus in Syria to Seville in Spain and from Carthage in North Africa to Corinth in Greece. Likewise, it is not hard to imagine the difficulties faced by a Roman Emperor who wished to impose his will across so many different cultures. But as different as they were, the lands that Rome ruled became one in many ways. It wasn't Latin, but one language could be used in every city of the Empire. Mile markers marched from Rome to the ends of the Empire along their Interstate highways. And soldiers under one command enforced laws that were enacted in Rome and kept a peace that came to be known as a Roman peace, the Pax Romana. It was the fullness of time.

We have seen the maps with the lines tracing the three missionary journeys of Paul all our Christian lives, but how faint an image of his travels these mere lines give us. It has been estimated that Paul travelled more than ten thousand miles on his journeys,[2] yet there is not one single reference in Paul's letters or the book of Acts to a scenic view or an interesting inn along the way or the route he took. On every journey he made, some of the trip involved a sea voyage, but Paul was not interested in describing in a journal the details about how he found a ship going where he wanted to go or how much it cost. We can only guess at the time his overland walks took by piecing together some hints about when he was in specific cities. There is not a word about how he spent his nights on the road, but there were very few motels,[3] so Paul and those with him must have spent many nights on the ground by the side of the road. How did they get their food? How did Paul carry his tent making tools? Did he

_____

[2] Ronald Hock (*The Social Context of Paul's Ministry: Tentmaking and Apostleship, 27*) has calculated that Paul traveled nearly ten thousand miles during his reported career, which put him on roads busy with "government officials, traders, pilgrims, the sick, letter-carriers, sightseers, runaway slaves, fugitives, prisoners, athletes, artisans, teachers, and students."

[3] There were inns on the major road but they were notorious for their lice and bandits. One is reminded of the "Master of the House" in Les Miserables who sings:

Charge 'em for the lice, extra for the mice
Two percent for looking in the mirror twice
Here a little slice, there a little cut
Three percent for sleeping with the window shut

15

travel with a donkey? How we wish he had jotted down some notes!

The Roman Roads

What do we know about travel in general in the Roman world? Let's start with the roads on which Paul walked. It is amazing that to this day some of these very roads are still in existence. The highways of the Roman Empire went right through the cities just as our old highways (like Route 66) did. If one began in Rome, he took the Appian Way across Italy to Brindisi on the Adriatic coast and crossed the Adriatic by ship landing at Dyrrachium (or at Apollonia). From there the Egnatian Way carried travelers all the way to what is today Istanbul. There were Roman mile markers on this road for 535 miles.[4] Travelers who wished to travel a southern route across what is today Turkey got off the road at Philippi and crossed the Agaean Sea by ship landing at Troas. The main road across Turkey was known as the Common Way[5] and began at Ephesus. This is the road Paul travelled on two of his journeys going the other way. It was four hundred miles as the crow flies from Ephesus to the junction

---

[4] Strabo, *Geography*, VII, 7, 4: "From Apollonia to Macedonia one travels the Egnatian Road, towards the east; it has been measured by Roman miles and marked by pillars as far as Cypsela and the Hebrus River — a distance of five hundred and thirty-five miles."

[5] "Across Asia Minor the "common route" *(koine hodos)* ran from Ephesus past Tralles, up the Maeander valley to Laodicea, to Apameia, Antioch by Pisidia, Philomelium, across Lycaonia to Iconium, down by Laranda and the Cilician Gates to Tarsus, then either to Antioch in Syria or across to Zeugma on the Euphrates." Wayne Meeks, *The First Urban Christians*, 17.

where the road turned south through the Cilician Gates (a famous pass through the Taurus mountains north of Tarsus) and of course, Paul didn't fly like the crow! From there it was forty-five miles through the mountains to the coastal highway that extended all the way to Harran and beyond in Mesopotamia.

A hundred years before Paul's lifetime these great roads were just trails. But Rome needed to move its armies and its couriers quickly and to make that possible they built roads. The roads they built lasted for centuries—some still are being used as the foundations for modern highways. Had Rome not built the roads it would have been impossible for Paul to take his Gospel across Galatia, Asia Minor and Macedonia and Greece. "The guiding thread for every history of earliest Christianity," writes Martin Hengel, "is the irresistible expansion of the Christian faith in the Mediterranean region during the first 120 years. That expansion was closely associated with personal mobility, both physical and social." [6] When the Gospel needed to be carried to the world in the fullness of time, it was carried on Roman roads.

The Roman Peace

A hundred years before Paul was born the Mediterranean Sea was nobody's ocean. Pirates roamed freely and unchecked. Travel by ship was hazardous at best. The roads were scarcely any safer. Foot travel was only possible for large groups that could protect themselves. Individuals or small groups could not use the roads. Gangs of thieves staked out their sections of the

---

[6] Meeks, *op. cit.*, 16

17

roads that existed and took what they wanted. The territory that would become the Roman Empire was just coming together, and it still consisted of a patchwork of regions with no government powerful enough to police the country sides. Had Paul lived a century or so earlier, the Gospel he carried in earthen vessels would have been hijacked on the seas and stolen on the roads. Letters Paul wrote could not have been delivered from church to church and city to city. It would have been unthinkable for a sizeable collection of money for the poor Christians of Jerusalem to be taken by sea and land from Macedonia to Israel.

The Romans changed all that and in so doing created a period of peace the likes of which the world has hardly seen before or since. They called it the Pax Romana—the Roman Peace—and it began with the accession of Augustus in 27 BC, which marked the end of the Roman Republic and its final civil wars, and lasted until 180 AD and the death of Marcus Aurelius. It came just in time for Paul and the Christian missionaries to make their way throughout the Roman empire with the Gospel. Looking back it almost seems providential—maybe it was.

"The Roman legal system, which forms the basis of many Western court systems today, unified the administration of justice in the courts throughout the provinces. The Legions patrolled the borders with success, and though there were still many foreign wars, the internal empire was free from major invasion, piracy, or social disorder on any grand scale. The empire, wracked with civil war for the last century of the Republic and for years following the Pax Romana, was largely free of large-scale power disputes. Only the year 69 AD, the so-called 'Year of the Four Emperors' following the fall of Nero and the Julio-Claudian line, interrupted nearly 200 years of civil order. Even this was only a minor hiccup in comparison to other eras. The arts and architecture flourished as well, along with commerce and the economy."[7]

The fullness of time was a time when people could move peacefully in any direction within the Roman Empire.

The Greek Language

Paul wrote letters and he sent them to churches in provinces that spoke many different languages and dialects. How could he do this? Even the casual tourist knows how difficult it can be just to ask a simple question when he is in a foreign city. I still remember with some pain a lady who stopped me on a street corner in Tel Aviv almost fifty years ago and asked for directions in her native tongue—and asked again in another language and yet again in a third tongue which she spoke. Unfortunately, I knew none of her languages and my ignorance was rewarded with a look of disdain from her. How is it that Paul managed not only to argue and communicate the Gospel to so many different places but to write lengthy letters of considerable theological depth to these cities?

---

[7] Quoted from Wikipedia at http://en.wikipedia.org /Pax_Romana.

The Romans aren't the only ones who deserve credit for Paul's ability to communicate so effectively. You see, Paul taught, argued, preached and wrote to his converts in just one language, and that language was Greek. Three hundred years before Paul was born Alexander the Great in an electrifying ten year process managed to defeat the mighty Persian armies and take control of everything from Athens to Babylon and beyond. "Alexander's legacy includes the cultural diffusion his conquests engendered. He founded some twenty cities that bore his name, most notably Alexandria in Egypt. Alexander's settlement of Greek colonists and the resulting spread of Greek culture in the east resulted in a new Hellenistic civilization..."[8] This is one time when the conquerors managed to transform the conquered in their own image—it often went the other way. After Alexander the whole literate world -if not every farmer in his village- spoke Greek. When Roman armies marched east to take over the vast empire Alexander had amassed, there was no need to change the culture. Romans spoke Latin in Rome, but across the empire they did business in Greek. In every single city which Paul visited the language in the streets was Greek along with the native tongue.

There is yet one more stream that fed this great river of culture on which the Gospel travelled. In one of those cities founded by Alexander the Great—the one in Egypt—Jews decided that the Bible (our Old Testament) needed to be in Greek

8 Quoted from the Wikipedia article on Alexander the Great located at http://en.wikipedia.org/wiki/Alexander_the_Great.

so Jews wherever they lived could read it. Hebrew and Aramaic were being lost by Jews swallowed up in the Greek world and with that loss came the loss of the divine word which meant so much to them. Sometime about a century and a half before Paul's birth the Jews in Alexandria put together a team of scholars that produced the first major version of the Bible—the Greek version known as the Septuagint.[9] This was Paul's Bible. He quotes it almost exclusively in his letters. It was used by the writers of our Gospels. It is commonplace for the quotations of the Old Testament in the New Testament not to agree fully with the text of our Old Testament. The reason for this is that our Old Testament goes back to the Hebrew while the New Testament writers for the most part quoted the Greek version. So not only was there one language available to Paul in which to preach, there was one Bible in Greek read by Jews all over the Roman world. There was a common foundation from which Paul could teach and reason. In the fullness of time they all spoke Greek.

The Jewish Diaspora

While no one would advocate inflicting pain and tragedy on a people in order to make them flourish, there have been cases where the near destruction of a people has caused them to multiply and flourish. The modern Jew may be the prime example! In the Bible one thinks of Israel, too, enslaved in Egypt for

---

9 The word Septuagint means "70." The legend said that seventy-two scholars miraculously translated the first five books of the Bible in a short time. The rest of the Bible was added later. The abbreviation for this version is LXX.

half a millennium or the terrible death-blow dealt to Israel by the Babylonians at the end of the Old Testament. Exile was a terrible thing to endure. But today, Jews all over the world use the Talmud which they know as the "Babylonian" Talmud. Exile in Babylon forced Jews to put their traditions in writing, and that made Judaism possible far beyond its exile. The exile in Babylon was not the first time Jews were pushed outward from Israel. Long before Israel fell to Babylon Jews had been forced to flee from their homeland by Assyrians. Just a few years after Jesus was crucified, the Romans killed thousands of Jews in putting down the Zealot's revolt of 66 A.D. that ended with the destruction of Herod's magnificent temple in 70 A.D. The shock waves of that assault sent Jews to the four points of the compass and seeded the world with their communities.

Thus it was, that when Paul took the Gospel from Antioch in Syria to Corinth in Greece he found Jews in every city he visited, and there was a synagogue in every city where he could present his case that Jesus was the Messiah. Many years earlier, after surviving a near death experience more than once Joseph spoke to his brothers who had sold him into slavery in Egypt. With a wisdom and compassion worthy of a great man, Joseph assured his brothers that he would not seek revenge on them for what they had done to him. "Fear not," he said, "for am I in the place of God? As for you, you meant evil against me; but God meant it for good, to bring it about that many people should be kept alive, as they are today."[10] Surely Babylon, Assyria, Syria, and Rome were enemies of Israel and dealt the Jews terrible blows—but because Jews were forced to flee, Judaism found a home in every city of the empire. They call this dispersion of the Jews the "Diaspora."[11] The word comes from a Greek word meaning "to scatter or to sow." Like seed cast from a farmers hand as he planted his crop, Jewish civilization was sown all over the Roman world. In many instances these seedlings were transplanted as Christians when the missionaries made their way from city to city.

Conclusion

It was indeed the fullness of time. The roads, the peace, the language, the Jewish Diaspora all made it possible for Good News to travel fast. Within thirty years of Jesus' crucifixion there was a Christian church in Rome half-way across the Roman world. The empire that made it possible to move so quickly did not survive, but the faith that sent missionaries across the sea and

---

[10] Genesis 50:19-20

[11] "In the first century some five to six million Jews were living in Diaspora, that is, more or less permanently settled outside Palestine. The Diaspora had begun at least as early as the deportations of the Babylonian exile, in the sixth century, and had been fed by subsequent dislocations through successive conquests of the homeland, but even more by voluntary emigration in search of better economic opportunities than the limited space and wealth of Palestine could afford. Consequently there was a substantial Jewish population in virtually every town of any size in the lands bordering the Mediterranean. Estimates run from 10 to 15 percent of the total population of a city—in the case of Alexandria, perhaps even higher." Meeks, *The First Urban Christians, 34.*

down the highways and byways of the empire found a home in the Roman world.

Chapter 2

Tarsus: The City that Gave Us Saul

As we begin our look at the cities associated with Paul, it is appropriate that we start with the city in which he was born. Tarsus gave us Saul. In later years he worked there and, we can assume, witnessed about Christ to all who would listen to him. After leaving Tarsus to join Barnabas in Antioch, Paul returned to Tarsus at least twice. On both his second and third missionary journeys Paul had to walk right through Tarsus—but he never mentions these visits in any letters still in existence. And speaking of letters, Paul did not write any letters to Tarsus, so its name is not as familiar as the names of cities like Philippi or Corinth. He may not have been able to start a church in Tarsus! Although there is today a Church of St. Paul in Tarsus it does not go back to the time of Paul. The first bishop of a church in Tarsus that can be verified is Helenus who dates to the two hundreds A.D. Nevertheless, even though Paul may not have been able to establish a church in Tarsus, the city played a major role in bringing us our thirteenth apostle. We can fill in some of the gaps in our knowledge about Tarsus, but there are still many things we would like to know about Paul's life in Tarsus. Neither Luke (in the book of Acts) nor Paul himself tells us much about his ministry in Tarsus after he became a Christian. So it's up to us to see what we can glean from others who lived in and around Tarsus in the first century.

Before we deal with Tarsus, let's talk about the two names by which we know this apostle. "Saul" obviously is a famous Hebrew name. The first king of Israel was named Saul! The name is related to the Hebrew word for "ask" indicating that the parents prayed for this child. Perhaps they had great hopes that he, too, would one day lead the nation. Saul was obviously the name he was given at birth. When, then, did he get the name "Paul?" We often assume that he got this name when he became a Christian on the Damascus Road, but this is most likely not the case. Paul lived in two worlds, the Hebrew and the Greek worlds. Apparently it was customary for Jews to have both a Hebrew and a Greek version of their names. They would have used their Greek name when they dealt with Gentiles outside the Jewish community. Paul's Greek name would have been "Paulus."

In the book of Acts, Luke uses the name Saul until the 13th chapter and then changes at that point to Paul. In that chapter, Paul and Barnabas sail to the island of Cyprus where they witnessed to the Roman Proconsul whose name was Sergius Paulus—that is, his name was "Paul." At this point, Luke described what came next by noting that " Saul, who is also called Paul"— that is, like the Proconsul-- confronted a magician. Luke began referring to Paul as "Paul" immediately after the conversion of the Roman official whose name was Paul. Luke never refers to Paul as Saul again except when he describes Paul's account of Jesus' words to him on the Damascus Road. Paul himself never refers to himself as "Saul" in any of his letters. How we wish that Luke had given us just a little more information! We know the apostle as "Paul" because Luke used that name for the rest of his book. We really don't know whether Paul continued to use both names or not, but presumably he did. Tarsus gave us the man we know by both names, Saul and Paul, but we are so used to calling him Paul it will be simpler to use that name even though for much of his pre-Christian life his friends and family would have called him Saul..

The Commercial Tarsus[12]

Paul was born not-like Jesus- in a village in Israel but in a city named Tarsus in a region known as Cilicia[13], a Roman province in what is today Turkey. We don't know the year, but he

---

[12] The headings and much of the information I'm using in this paper come from a very helpful book by Bruce Chilton, *Rabbi Paul,* published by Doubleday in 2004.

[13] "Cilicia as a whole consists of two parts: the inaccessible western area of the Taurus mountains, also known as "rough Cilicia", and the eastern plains, which are dominated by the rivers Cydnus, Sarus and Pyramis and are rich in cereals. The Taurus [mountains form] the region's northern border. Here, we find the Cilician Gate, a pass that connects the plain with Cappadocia in the north. To the south, the Mediterranean sea is Cilicia's neighbor, and the region knew (and knows) close contacts with Cyprus. In the east the Syrian gates are the connection with Syria and Mesopotamia." Jona Lendering, "Cilicia," at http://www.livius. org/cg-cm/cilicia/cilicia.html.

was probably born a few years after Jesus—5 A.D is a reasonable guess. Presumably Paul's father was a tentmaker; since it was normal for a son to work in the same trade as his father, and Paul tells us that he himself was a tentmaker. That means that Saul's family was part of what made Tarsus famous—they were in business in Tarsus. The region of Cilicia was famous for its black wool and the tents made from it. Apparently Saul's family had become wealthy perhaps because of the demand for the goat hair tents they made. By virtue of its location at a major "interstate" intersection, Tarsus became a major commercial center. Ships unloaded their wares at the dock in the lagoon which lay between Tarsus and the sea. Caravans of traders from Syria and beyond came in a steady stream from the east and set up their tents in Tarsus to sell their goods—tents that Saul's family sold and re-paired. Overland traffic from Macedonia and Ephesus descend-ed from the Taurus mountains through what is known as the Ci-lician Gates just thirty miles north of Tarsus. A narrow road had been carved out of the sheer rock wall of the mountain. There was only one road south through the mountains and it led to Tarsus. Today the main highway follows this exact same route. Thus Tarsus was the largest city in the region and the capital of Cilicia early in the first century.

Paul began his life in a large city. It should not surprise us, then, that he spent most of his adult life in Roman cities with Greek cultures much like what he knew from his home town of

Tarsus.[14] There is not a word in Paul's letters or the Book of Acts about Paul's stops in small towns! Jesus and Paul could not have had any more different experiences. Jesus grew up in a tiny village in Galilee next door to a big city, Sepphoris; Paul grew up in the city. Jesus grew up in an Aramaic community; Paul was at home in a Greek speaking world. Jesus read the Bible in Hebrew; Paul read the Bible in Greek. Jesus saw his mission as one only to the children of Israel; Paul believed his call was to take salvation to the Gentiles. The big business center of Tarsus in which Paul grew up had much to do with shaping both his Judaism and his Christianity.

Where Was Tarsus in Cilicia?

The Mediterranean Sea is not square, but if we think of it as a rectangle, Israel and Syria would be on the east end. Italy, Greece and Turkey occupy the north shore. Egypt and North Africa form the southern shore of the Mediterranean. Spain closes off the west end. Tarsus, the city of Paul's birth, was just around the corner from Syria on the eastern end of Turkey. At the time of Paul's birth Tarsus was the capital city of Cilicia. The city was connected to the Mediterranean some ten miles away by

---

[14] "It is striking how strongly oriented his later missionary activity was toward the metropolitan areas and provincial capitals (Antioch on the Orontes, Thessalonica, Ephesus, Rome) and Roman colonies (Pisidian Antioch, Iconium, Lystra, Troas, Philippi, Corinth). It is hardly likely that the communities awaiting Paul in Spain were Jewish (cf. Rom. 15:24, 28) (§15.5.3); on the contrary, this population was one of the most strongly Romanized in the Empire, and one that spoke Latin almost exclusively." Rainer Riesner, *Paul's Early Period* (Grand Rapids: Eerdmans, 1998), 149.

the river Cydnus. It had a nice lagoon that allowed ships to sail up the river and into the city making it a center of commerce.[15] Much of the grain that fed Rome came from Alexandria in Egypt. The grain ships often hugged the coast line and found a sheltered harbor at Tarsus. The city was actually some ten miles from the Mediterranean shore line and dominated the coastal region—the region known as "Smooth Cilicia" as distinct from the mountainous "Rough Cilicia" to the north of the city. All traffic that moved from Mesopotamia and Syria to the west had to move through Tarsus. At Tarsus the road turned due north to go through the Taurus Mountains. The passage through the mountains was known as the Cilician Gates, a geographical landmark known to all travelers that was some 30 miles from Tarsus. Today, Tarsus has been swallowed up by the larger cities of Adana and Mersin.

---

[15] It was in this lagoon that Anthony met Cleopatra in one of the most famous "dates" in history, later commemorated by Shakespeare. The love story of Mark Antony (Marcus Antonius) and Cleopatra began here in 41 B.C. Some eight years before, Cleopatra had had herself delivered to Caesar in Alexandria by a merchant, wrapped in a carpet. This time she arranged a parade. She had built for herself a barge with fittings in gold and silver and equipped with purple silk sails. The vessel 's crew, young boys and girls, were dressed as gods and goddesses. The sound of music and scent of rich perfumes reached across the water to the Tarsians who had flocked to the Cydnus ' banks. Cleopatra herself reclined beneath a canopy of cloth of gold. This was the beginning of a love story, which lasted about a decade, with the well – known fatal end. Among many things, which Antony would bestow on his beloved after a few years, was the cedar - rich mountains of Rough Cilicia, which was a major source of timber for ship building for the Roman world.

The Pagan Tarsus

If the commercial side of Tarsus which exposed Paul to the world outside Israel prepared him for a ministry to cities, the pagan culture of Tarsus prepared him for a ministry to Gentiles. Many years into his ministry Luke tells us that Paul walked the streets of Athens and saw statues of many gods, among them one to an "Unknown God." Many Jews reared in a family that kept the purity laws of Judaism would have been immobilized by the uncleanness that surrounded Paul in the Greek world. He was not. He had grown up knowing the stories of the Greek gods. He had seen up close the great celebrations associated with the ancient religions that provided the world view for the majority population of Cilicia. The region of Cilicia had been controlled by Hittites, Persians, Greeks, Seleucids and Romans over the centuries. All of them left traces of their faiths in the religion of Tarsus. "In the growth of an ancient city no religious fact was ever wholly lost. When immigrants or colonists settled there, they brought their own religion with them, but they did not destroy the previously existing religion any more than they exterminated the older population."[16] Because of the influence of the eastern powers, the local god of Tarsus would have been related to the Baals Paul knew about from the Old Testament. The people of Tarsus called this god Baal-Tarz or "the Lord of Tarsus." They also called him Tarku.

---

[16] William M. Ramsay, *The Cities of St. Paul* (Grand Rapids, MI: Baker Book House, 1960 [reprinted from the 1907 edition]), 138.

"Tarku had been the people's god since before time could be reckoned. He wore an Anatolian headdress as he rode standing on his celestial beast, holding a blossoming flower in his right hand and a battle ax in his left, sword and bow case strapped to the same side of his body. He conveyed fertility, protection, the commanding strength of youth. Offspring of a father-god and a goddess, every spring he was carried to his temple, and there he was burned in effigy. As the flames leaped up to heaven in the midst of sacrifice and incense, he became a god, and Tarku's apotheosis—symbolized by an eagle at the apex of his pyramid—brought the promise that the spring planting would be successful, that another year would see Tarsus healthy and prosperous."[17]

Paul and his Jewish family would not have participated in the great procession in which Tarku was carried to the temple each year, but he could no more have been ignorant of it than a modern day Jewish family could miss Santa Claus. Bruce Chilton notes that "his own words show how deeply [the great procession] shaped his religious consciousness. In one of his rhetorical flourishes, he describes himself as being led in procession amidst clouds of incense, on the way to a personal apotheosis (2 Corinthians 2:14-163):

17 Bruce Chilton, *Rabbi Paul*, 10

Thanks to God, who always leads us in procession in the Messiah, and manifests the fragrance of his knowledge through us in every place, because we are Messiah's aroma for God among those who are being saved and among those who are perishing, either a fragrance of death for death or a fragrance of life for life."[18]

The Jewish Tarsus

Paul was born to Jewish parents whom he says were Pharisees, that is, they believed in living by all the rules of purity in the Old Testament. Thus Paul was born into a very conservative Jewish family albeit one which did not live in the land of Israel.[19] We are given no information about how many generations this family had lived in Cilicia nor do we know why they were there. We do know that a large group of Jewish families—some 2,000-- was relocated to this region by Antiochus III, the ruler of the Seleucid (Syrian) kingdom in 210 B. C. Paul's ancestors may have been one of these families. Apparently Paul's family had lived in this region for several generations because by the time Paul was born the family had attained Roman citizenship. This

---

[18] *Ibid.*, 11

[19] Some Jewish scholars argue that Paul was willing to accept Gentiles because he was from the Diaspora which they claim was generally more lax in regard to keeping the Law than Jews in Israel itself. Paul himself says he was ultra conservative.

would have placed the family in the upper social strata of the city and the region.

We have little direct information about the Jewish section of Tarsus in the first century, but there is a lot known about such communities in other cities. In every Roman city, citizens were encouraged to form groups which were primarily social clubs but varied in size and structure. " It seems to have been possible for almost anyone to "gather" *(synagein* is the word often used) a group of friends, relatives, neighbors, or working associates, draw up a constitution, find a meeting place, and declare themselves the Association *(thiasos, synodos, eranos,* or the like) of N."[20] The Greek word for "gather" above is very close to the word the Jews used for their meeting places—"synagogue"—so it would be natural for the Greeks and Romans to view the Jewish communities as just another "association" like other groups formed. Indeed one Roman official recorded a petition from the Jews of Sardis in 49 B.C. which demonstrates how the Jews were regarded:

> "Jewish citizens of ours have come to me and pointed out that from the earliest times they have had an association *[synodos]* of their own in accordance with their native laws *[kata tous patrious nontous]* and a place *[topos]* of

[20] Wayne Meeks, *The First Urban Christians* (New Haven: Yale University Press, 2003 [Second Edition]), 31

their own, in which they decide their affairs
and controversies with one another."[21]
Thus the Jewish communities like the one into which Paul was
born had a favored and protected existence in most Roman cities
including the right of self governance inside the community.

"The Jews of Tarsus could freely pursue trades, tent-making among them. This skilled craft required expertise and tools—and therefore investment in people and material—to work the leather and felt from which tents were made. But the investment offered excellent prospects: any army or caravan of traders had need of professionals to get their camps set up and keep them in good repair. Travel meant wear and tear, even on the heavy materials the best tents were made from, so contractors in the business, keeping a row of shops with tenements for a couple dozen workers and slaves upstairs, were richly rewarded."[22]

But what kind of Judaism was practiced in these communities far from Jerusalem. Many Jews today assume that the Judaism of the disapora communities—the communities of Jews outside Israel—practiced an inferior brand of the faith. They sometimes conclude that Paul would never

---

[21] Meeks, *op. cit.*, 34
[22] Chilton, *op. cit.*, 12. The Anatolia News Agency announced in 2012 that a second Jewish synagogue had been found in the region of ancient Cilicia. A previous discovery of a synagogue was made in 2009. These discoveries underscore the presence of Jews in the region in Paul's lifetime.

have become a Christian had he not been influenced by his more liberal version of Judaism. There is no doubt that Judaism far from the Temple was somewhat different from that in the land of Israel itself. For one thing, the Jews of the diaspora read their Old Testament in Greek rather than in Hebrew. Almost all of Paul's quotations of the Old Testament come from the Septuagint—the Greek translation. But Paul defends himself against charges that his Judaism was watered down by noting his conservative Jewish background and his training in Jerusalem itself under the tutelage of a famous Rabbi, Gamaliel. He classed himself as a Pharisee. There may be no way to tell for sure what course Paul's life would have taken had he been born in Jerusalem, but it is surely neither accurate nor fair to assume that no one outside Israel could be as devout as those within.[23]

The Pauline Tarsus

Tarsus was an ancient city, a commercial city, a city that had accumulated religions for centuries and kept them all, a Jewish city—but was it Paul's city? What contact with Tarsus did Paul himself have? We know he was born in the city but we do not know when he left for Jerusalem and we don't know whether his family remained in Tarsus after he

---

[23] I remember in this context an afternoon spent in the summer of 1965 in the home of the first Prime Minister of Israel, Mr. David Ben Gurion, when he was asked if a person could be a good Jew and live in New York City. Mr. Ben Gurion responded with great vigor that it was not possible!

went to Jerusalem although it is assumed they did. So what can we know?

Citizenship

Not only was Paul born in Tarsus, he was born a citizen of Tarsus. That may not sound like two different things to us, but it was normal for a person to live in a Roman city like Tarsus and not have citizenship. Citizenship was granted by the Roman government and families who had citizenship would have belonged to the upper social strata of any city. Paul says that "'I am a Jew, from Tarsus in Cilicia, a citizen of no ordinary city" (NIV Acts 21:39). He also revealed that he was a citizen by birth, that is, he did not buy his citizenship nor was it awarded to him for some service.[24]. Roman citizenship made it illegal to punish a person without a proper investigation of the circumstances. Citizenship apparently did not always save a person from illegal treatment. Paul notes that the officials of Philippi in Macedonia "have beaten us publicly, un-condemned, men who are Roman

---

[24] "Some scholars speculate that Paul may be a descendant of some of those who were promised free citizenship if they moved to the Cilician city in 171 BCE. Another claim for the citizenship ancestry of Paul can be found in some who raise the possibility that Paul's father or grandfather helped Marc Antony (and thus Rome) during Cleopatra's renowned visit to Tarsus in 41 BCE. The historian Strabo mentions the splendor of the event, as Cleopatra sailed her gilded barge in the Cyndus into the city. In addition, there is reason to believe that Antony and Octavian used some resources of the city in their struggle against Brutus and Cassius, who they later defeated at Philippi in Macedonia. Some have even suggested that a tent maker's gift could have been repaid in citizenship (cp. Acts 18:3), though this is mere speculation."
http://www.enjoyturkey.com/Tours/ Interest/Biblicals/tarsus.htm.

citizens…" (Acts 16:37). But at least once Paul's citizenship may have saved his life. When he was arrested in Jerusalem, bound with thongs and about to be whipped, Paul said to the Centurion in charge, "Is it lawful for you to scourge a man who is a Roman citizen and un-condemned?" (Acts 22:25). When questioned by the commanding officer about his status, Paul proudly noted that "I was born a citizen." (Acts 22:28). Two years later after being held prisoner by the Roman governor, Paul used his citizenship to appeal for a trial before the Roman Emperor himself—a safeguard that every Roman citizen in the empire had. Paul's birth in Tarsus as a Roman citizen played a huge role in his life later on.

Childhood Education

The Tarsus Paul grew up in was a college town. The Greek historian Strabo wrote that " The people at Tarsus have devoted themselves so eagerly, not only to philosophy, but also to the whole round of education in general, that they have surpassed Athens, Alexandria, or any other place that can be named where there have been schools and lectures of philosophers.[25] Needless to say, coming in third behind Athens and Alexandria is not bad. So Paul started life in an intellectual city as well as a city flush with wealth from commerce. We have no indication that Paul went to school in Tarsus or actually was influenced by its philosophers, but he clearly was at home with Greek rhetoric and

---

[25] Strabo, *Geography* 14.5.13

this stood him in good stead as he thought about the Christian faith.

Education for Jewish boys was centered in the synagogue with the rabbi as the teacher. According to Judah ben Tema, "At five years old [one is fit] for the [study of] Scripture, at ten years for [the study of] the Mishnah, at thirteen for [the fulfilling of] the commandments, at fifteen for the Talmud, …"Avot 5:21). Paul says he studied in Jerusalem under Gamaliel, a famous first century rabbi whom Luke says counseled his Sanhedrin colleagues to allow Peter and the Christians to speak.[26] Gamaliel was the grandson of the even more famous rabbi, Hillel. Paul would have studied with Gamaliel at least from the age of 15 onward but got his early basic education as a Jew in Tarsus.

Paul's Later Life in Tarsus

According to the book of Acts, Paul went back to Tarsus some three years after his conversion on the Damascus Road. Following a visit to Jerusalem to see Peter and James, Luke says he went into the region of Syria (Damascus?) and Cilicia. If he went to Cilicia, it can be assumed that he went to Tarsus for that was both his home and the capital of Cilicia. How long was he in Tarsus after his conversion? It is notoriously difficult to determine this with any certainty, but there is a period of several years—perhaps as many as eight years—in which he lived in Tar-

---

[26] Acts 5:39: "…if (the Christian preaching) is of God, you will not be able to overthrow them. You might even be found opposing God."

sus. We never hear of a church there so presumably Paul's preaching and teaching in Tarsus did not convince many of his home town to accept Christ.

We have no references to Paul's immediate family during this period. Were his parents still alive? We don't know. If they were still alive what was their reaction to Paul's Christian witness? We don't know, but Paul himself may have given us a clue. He says to the Philippians that "I have suffered the loss of all things, and count them as refuse, in order that I may gain Christ..." (Philippians 3:8). We know that Paul was dependent on his own labor as a tent maker and on the support of churches like the one in Philippi to pay his expenses. He clearly had very little income as an apostle. It would seem logical that Paul's family had disinherited him and that he had lost his share of the family fortune. We can only wonder if he was actually rejected by his parents and spent those years in Tarsus after his conversion in isolation from his family.

Tarsus and the Missionary Journeys

The first missionary journey of Paul, Barnabas and John Mark bypassed Tarsus because the group took a boat from Syria to Cyprus and then entered what is today Turkey far to the west of Tarsus, so he did not go through his home town on that trip. However, on both the second and third journeys, he walked overland through Syria and turned west to go through Cilicia. He would have stopped in Tarsus on both trips before heading north through the Cilician Gates to the interior of Asia Minor. He does not mention either of these stops in any of his letters that we have. Neither does Luke tell us anything about him stopping in Tarsus; Luke covers the entire trip from Antioch in Syria to the interior of Turkey on the second trip in just one sentence: "And he went through Syria and Cilicia strengthening the churches" (Acts 15:41). A similar one sentence description covered Paul's walk through Cilicia on the third trip: "After spending some time there (in Antioch) he departed and went from place to place through the region of Galatia and Phrygia, strengthening all the disciples" (Acts 18:23). Apparently, Luke was much more familiar with Paul's work further west and did not have detailed information about what Paul did at the beginning of these trips. We can hardly help being curious, however, about Paul's return trips through Tarsus. Did he have family there to visit? Was he welcomed by them or shunned? Did he convince anyone in Tarsus to become a Christian? Was there a church there when he left to go back to Antioch? But we have no answers to these questions. There is a gap in our knowledge of Christianity in Tarsus from Paul's time to the third century A.D. when there was a church with a bishop there.

Conclusion

Jesus once noted that "a prophet is not without honor, except in his own country and among his own kin, and in his own house" (Mark 6:4). That may well be the way it was with Paul, too. Everywhere he went he left Christians and churches—

41

except Tarsus. But while he may not have left evidence of himself in this ancient place, the place surely left its mark on him. Its Jewish community grounded him in the scriptures. Its market place gave him a trade with which to sustain himself when he "suffered the loss of all things." Its location at a major crossroad between east and west allowed him to interact comfortably with Gentiles. Its long immersion in Hellenistic culture made him fluent in Greek and philosophy. Its place in the Roman world pointed Paul's ministry to "the end of the earth" far beyond Jerusalem, Judea and Samaria. Indeed, Luke was very prescient when he ended the story of Paul's life with Paul in jail but the Gospel "let loose in the world." And it all started in Tarsus.

Chapter 3

Damascus: The City That Gave Us Paul

If Tarsus gave us Saul, it was surely Damascus that gave us Paul—at least as we know him. He already had the name "Paul" before he became a Christian on the Damascus Road. "Paul" was the Apostle's Greek name, his business name, which he used outside the Jewish community. His name did not change because of his experience on the Damascus Road, but everything else about his life did. Neither Luke (in the book of Acts) nor Paul himself tells us a great deal about the city of Damascus, but it was the place where Paul began his ministry as a Christian. Tarsus was old but Damascus is truly ancient. Mark Twain may have said it best:

> "...no recorded event has occurred in the world but Damascus was in existence to receive the news of it. Go back as far as you will into the vague past, there was always a Damascus."[27]

We'll look at the role Damascus played in Israel's history, trace what we can of the formation of a Jewish community in the city, look at the modern city and the sites associated with Paul, see if we can figure out Paul's movements immediately after his conversion and, finally, note the times Luke does not tell us

---

[27] Mark Twain, *Innocents Abroad* (1869) 457

about when Paul must have been in Damascus. Last week we learned that Paul identified the time of his life as "the fullness of time" when God acted to reveal himself in Christ. Paul's lifetime coincided with the Pax Romana when all things came together to make it possible for the Gospel to penetrate the whole Mediterranean world because that world was unified into one kingdom with one language and Jewish communities everywhere who already knew the Old Testament. In many other periods it would have been unthinkable for there to be a Jewish community in Damascus—the capital of Israel's hated enemy, Syria. But the story of Paul's remarkable apostleship begins in the home of a Jew named Judas on a street called Straight in the city of Damascus. Let's see what we can learn about the setting for Paul's story.

Where Is Damascus?

Damascus is some 135 miles north of Jerusalem as the crow flies, but modern political realities have both shrunk that distance and widened it dramatically. The distance is so small that modern jet fighter planes can span the gap in a matter of minutes. But the alienation of the two countries has pushed them so far apart that it is impossible to simply drive from one city to the other. As this presentation is being written[28] Damascus has been on our news every evening for months as a civil war is being waged in the attempt to overthrow the current regime,

---

[28] January, 2017

44

but seeing the pictures does not help us get a good feel for where this city is. Let's start with some geography.

Far to the north of Jerusalem on a clear day one can see the snow capped peak of Mt. Hermon. Mt. Hermon is the highest mountain in the Anti-Lebanon Range. Damascus is at the foot of the eastern slopes of the Anti-Lebanon Range, situated at the base of Mt. Qassioun. Mt. Qassioun towers over Damascus and offers visitors and resident families alike a delightful view of the ancient city at dusk. It is said that as Mohammed approached the crest of Mt. Qassioun he stopped to behold the magnificent scene before him but turned back without entering the city. He explained that a man could only enter Paradise once!

Damascus served as a major stop for caravans from the east and west travelling the Silk Road. It has always been a great trading city and the city was famous for its crafts and wealth. The best testimony to this is the term "Damascene" which was used to describe the best silk, sword and, indeed, anything that is the symbol of quality and fashion.[29] Like Tarsus, Damascus had the good fortune to be located where the major routes met and to have plentiful and perennial water. Rivers flow out of the mountains and make Damascus a veritable oasis. Na'aman the Leper from Damascus who came to Elishah to be healed was disappointed with Israel's little river (the Jordan) and exclaimed

---

[29] Damascene is now most often associated with Toledo, Spain but the term originated in Damascus.

"'Are not Aba'na and Pharpar, the rivers of Damascus, better than all the waters of Israel? Could I not wash in them, and be clean?' So he turned and went away in a rage."[30] The river called "Aba'na" in this text is the Barada river which actually flows through Damascus. The other river, called "Pharpar" here, is to the south of the city. Although Mark Twain was not impressed by the rivers of Damascus ("mere creeks"), he still wrote after visiting the city that "So long as its waters remain to it—so long will Damascus live."[31]

Damascus and Jews

Damascus and Jerusalem, Syria and Israel, were natural competitors and fierce enemies for as long as Judah and Israel existed although there is a reference in I Kings to an agreement that allowed the two countries to have "bazaars" in each other's cities.[32] One of the most memorable stories about Syria and Israel begins, "For three years Syria and Israel continued without war. But in the third year, Jehoshaphat the king of Judah came down to the king of Israel [Ahab]. And the king of Israel said to his servants, 'Do you know that Ramoth-gilead belongs to us...and he said to Jehoshaphat, 'Will you go with me to bat-

---

[30] 2 Kings 5:12

[31] Mark Twain, *Innocents Abroad*, 457.

[32] I Kings 20:34: "And Ben-Hadad said to him [Ahab], "The cities which my father took from your father I will restore; and you may establish bazaars for yourself in Damascus, as my father did in Samaria."

tle?"[33] To make a long story short, Jehoshaphat insisted on praying about the matter and asked that a prophet be consulted outside the 400 prophets that Ahab had on the payroll. Ahab brought in Micaiah ben Imlah even though he exclaimed, "I hate him for he never prophecies good concerning me." Sure enough Micaiah, when asked whether the battle to retake Ramoth-gilead should go forward, first said "Go up to Ramoth-gilead and triumph…"—but the tone of his voice made it clear he didn't mean it. When pressed he said, "I saw all Israel scattered upon the mountains, as sheep that have no shepherd…" and that's the way the story ended. Ahab was struck by a chance arrow and mortally wounded, and Israel's army was scattered.

Because of this long standing enmity between Syria and Israel, it is somewhat surprising to learn that there was a Jewish community in Damascus in Paul's day. We know this both from secular histories of Damascus and from our New Testament. Sometime after the stoning of Stephen in Jerusalem which caused Christians to leave that city, Paul is described as asking for letters from the Jewish leadership in Jerusalem giving him authority to identify Christians in Damascus.

> "But Saul, still breathing threats and murder against the disciples of the Lord, went to the high priest and asked him for letters to the synagogues at Damascus, so that if he found any belonging to

---

[33] See I Kings 22 for the whole story.

the Way, men or women, he might bring them bound to Jerusalem." (Acts 9:1-2)

The reference is to "synagogues" in the plural so Damascus had more than one synagogue about the year 31 A.D. The Jewish historian Josephus suggests that there were some 10,000 Jewish men in the city of Damascus.[34] This would place the total Jewish population at more than double that number. If this is correct, Damascus would have had a major Jewish population and since it was by this time a Greek speaking part of the Roman Empire it apparently was one place to which the Christian "Hellenists" migrated after the death of Stephen.[35]

Damascus and Nabataeans

Paul's account of his Damascus Road experience in Galatians says that immediately after his encounter with Christ "I went away into Arabia; and again I returned to Damascus" (Gal 1:17). We automatically equate Arabia with Saudi Arabia which lies far to the south of Damascus, but in Paul's time Arabia extended all the way into Damascus. Arabia in Paul's time referred

---

[34] Martin Hengel and Anna Maria Schwemer, *Paul Between Damascus and Antioch* (Louisville, KY: Westminster Press, 1997) 54.

[35] See Acts 6:1: "Now in these days when the disciples were increasing in number, the Hellenists murmured against the Hebrews because their widows were neglected in the daily distribution." The Hellenist Christians were those who spoke Greek. The seven deacons selected to address this situation all had Greek names: Stephen, Philip, Prochorus, Nicanor, Timon, Parmenas and Nicolaus. The last mentioned, Nicolaus, is specifically said to have been a "proselyte." He was not a Jew by birth but had adopted the Jewish faith.

to the territory of the Nabataeans whose capital was the famous rock carved city of Petra. Thus when Paul says he went away into Arabia it means he left the city and went east into the desert region but not necessarily a long way. We don't know what Paul did while he was in Nabataean territory, but apparently the king of the Nabataeans, Aretas, instructed his governor who ruled Damascus to arrest Paul. Paul tells us this in 2 Corinthians 11:32 and links this attempt to arrest him to his escape over the city wall in a basket. Some conclude that Paul's first preaching to non-Jews was done in Arabia with the Nabataeans.

Damascus and Paul

One of the things that complicates our understanding of Paul's life is that Luke's account of Paul's movements sometimes conflicts with statements that Paul himself made in his letters. These conflicting statements have led many historians to prefer Paul's first-hand knowledge as giving the more accurate account. On the other hand, there is obviously a lot of information in Luke which is very accurate and sometimes Luke is the only one who tells us about Paul's actions. Acts 9 is Luke's first account of Paul's experience on the Damascus Road. He tells this same basic story two more times (Acts 22 and 26) as he describes Paul's arrest in Jerusalem and his imprisonment in Caesarea. The accounts are not exactly alike and this is understandable given the occasions on which they were said to be spoken. The events that connect Paul with the city of Damascus in these accounts are: his experience on the road to Damascus, his initial introduction to the Christians in Damascus, his flight from Damascus and, perhaps, an extended ministry in Damascus before going to Jerusalem for his first meeting with Peter and James. Let's look at each of these.

On The Road

There are more questions about Paul's Damascus Road experience than there are answers by far. How long after Stephen's death was this experience? Why here? Should we call this a conversion or a call? Was the crucial moment on the road when the light blinded him or in the house when the scales fell from his eyes and the light shone in?

The question of when this event took place is complicated. Luke does not tell us when it happened and neither does Paul. Obviously, the Damascus Road experience occurred some time after Jesus' crucifixion and Stephen's martyrdom. It is generally conceded today that Jesus was crucified on April 7, 30 A.D.[36] How long after this was it when Stephen was stoned? While there is no consensus today on the date of Stephen's death, it seems probable that it happened within a year or two of the crucifixion, possibly in 32 A.D. In support of this dating there is a very old tradition that Jesus appeared to disciples over a period of a year and a half. Paul asserted that Jesus' appearance to him on the Damascus Road was the last of the appearances of

---

[36] Rainer Riesner, *Paul's Early Period* (Grand Rapids: Eerdmans, 1998) 58

Jesus.[37] When these two strands are combined it is suggested that Paul encountered Jesus on the road to Damascus in the year 32 A.D.[38]

If indeed the death of Stephen which was witnessed by Paul (Acts 7:58) was fresh on Paul's mind as he made that trip toward Damascus we may be able to answer our second question of "Why here?" Why did Jesus break in upon Paul on the Damascus Road. Why not in Jerusalem? Perhaps the answer lies in the effect that terrible stoning had on the heart and mind of the young rabbi at whose feet the mob laid their garments as they hurled their hatred at Stephen along with their stones. Soon after witnessing the event he sought a more active role in the persecution of Christians. Luke says he "ravaged" the church "entering house after house" in Jerusalem and physically dragging Christians out of their homes. The request to be authorized to do the same in Damascus where Christians had apparently fled sounds like a ramping up of the intensity of Paul's anger. But apparently on that hundred mile walk to the north, he began to see what he was doing in a different light. By the time he reached the outskirts of the city his heart was ready for a revelation and it came in a blinding moment, literally. The voice he heard did not tell him anything new but it put him on high alert for what was to

---

[37] I Corinthians 15:8 :"Last of all , as to one untimely born, he appeared also to me."

[38] Riesner, 66. Other scholars conclude that the year was 33 or 34 A.D. The matter is complex.

happen next. The voice said he would be told what to do in Damascus.

Did Paul cease to be a Jew on the road to Damascus? Was he converted from Jew to Christian? Well, certainly he became a Christian but he never ceased being a Jew. He was a Jew who had a new understanding of what the scripture was saying and what God was doing.[39] It may well be better to say that the Damascus Road experience was his call. In ancient Israel, Isaiah's lips were seared with a hot coal; on the road to Damascus it was Paul's heart that was touched.

We know that the blinded Paul was taken to the home of a man named Judas—obviously a Jew---who lived on Straight Street in Damascus. There he prayed and waited to be told what to do. Isn't it amazing how things work out! Surely in the tight knit Jewish community of Damascus word spread fast about what had happened. People knew about Paul—Saul as he was known to them. Surely in the Christian community the word spread even more quickly. One of those Christians had a vision and it doubtless picked up much of what Ananias had heard on the street. He knew where Saul was. He knew why he had come. But he also had heard that Jesus had spoken to Saul. He knew that God was at work. He knew he had to go. What a risk he took! What a scene in that bedroom on Straight Street in

---

[39] Riesner, 397. Riesner quotes C. Dietzfelbinger who wrote: "...one finds that the Damascus-experience is chronologically the place forcing Paul to rethink the Torah. *From the very outset*, then the problem of the law had to dominate his theology..."

Damascus. He touched him like Jesus touched a leper, and the first word he said was "Brother!" And then he confessed that the same Jesus who had appeared to Paul on the road had sent him to help Paul see again. And it happened.

In the Church

I wonder who baptized Paul. Luke only gives this event one line: " Then he rose and was baptized, and took food and was strengthened" (Acts 9:18-19). Who witnessed it? How many Christians were there in Damascus who were willing to identify themselves to Paul. In whose house was the church? Was there a synagogue that had several members who had been convinced that Jesus was the Messiah? These are questions we just can't answer but can hardly keep from asking.

Luke tells us that Paul spent "several days" "with the disciples at Damascus." He used his time to make the rounds of the synagogues "proving that Jesus was the Christ." We can imagine the stir that this caused in the Jewish community. Some (many?) were persuaded by Paul who was obviously a very bright and gifted debater as well as a superbly educated rabbi. The leadership of the Jewish community would have become more and more incensed as some agreed with Paul. It was doubtless in these very early debates in the synagogues of Damascus that the theology of Paul the Christian was shaped, a theology that he would carry around the Roman world in the following thirty years.

Over the Wall

It is just at this juncture that things get murky. Paul's own statements about his movements are very difficult (possibly impossible) to reconcile with Luke's account. Luke says that a plot to kill Paul led to his escape over the wall of Damascus in a basket. Luke says only that this occurred "many days" after Paul's Damascus Road experience. Luke attributes the plot to kill Paul to "the Jews."

Paul himself says that "the governor under King Aretas guarded the city of Damascus in order to seize me…" (2 Corinthians 11:32). Paul's statement seems to place responsibility for the plot to kill him not on the Jews but on the Nabateans who controlled the city of Damascus. It would be surprising if the Jews who were outraged by Paul's change of sides were not behind the retaliation against him, but perhaps the two statements can be understood as complementing each other. The police force of the government apparently cooperated with the Jewish leadership just as the Romans did in Jerusalem when Jesus was crucified.

In the letter to the Galatians, Paul wrote that after his experience on the road "I went away into Arabia; and again I returned to Damascus" (Galatians 1:17) Since the Nabateans controlled "Arabia" this may explain the involvement of the Nabatean governor, but it is difficult to know how much time was involved. Perhaps Paul spent as much as three years in Damascus before the episode described here. We cannot really tell.

Conclusion

If Tarsus gave us a person named Saul, Damascus really is responsible for the man we know of as Paul even if his name was not actually changed there. It was in Damascus that his heart was convicted of his sin, his life was given a new direction, his theology was shaped on the anvil of the debates with Jewish leaders, and, perhaps, it was here that he made his first presentations to non-Jews in the form of the Nabateans who also lived in Damascus. What a tremendous difference this city and its Christians made. It was this Paul who--determined to know nothing except Jesus Christ and him crucified—did the serious thinking necessary to shape our understanding of what God did in Christ. It was he who also at the very risk of his life and through suffering inflicted in so many different ways actually took that message of Christ to the streets of the Roman Empire and won hearts and minds in every city he touched.

Chapter 4

Antioch: The City That Gave Us Christians

The city of Antioch doesn't appear in the book of Acts until chapter 11, but its story begins in chapter 2! On that first Pentecost when Peter preached about Jesus to the masses who had come from all over the Jewish world, Luke tells us that people from many places heard the Gospel in their own language for the first time. Notice the places from which he said those Jews came: Parthians, Medes, Elamites and residents of Mesopotamia, Judea and Cappadocia, Pontus, Asia, Phrygia, Pamphylia, Egypt, Cyrene, Rome, Crete and Arabia. [40] The first four names never play a role in the book of Acts again. Perhaps Luke intended to tell the story of the eastward movement of the Gospel in another volume of his book. Most of the rest of the places are west of Jerusalem and with the exception of Egypt all are places Paul went. And all of them have something to do with Antioch.

---

[40]Acts 2: [5]Now there were dwelling in Jerusalem Jews, devout men from every nation under heaven. … [8] And how is it that we hear, each of us in his own native language? [9] Par'thians and Medes and E'lamites and residents of Mesopota'mia, Judea and Cappado'cia, Pontus and Asia, [10] Phryg'ia and Pamphyl'ia, Egypt and the parts of Libya belonging to Cyre'ne, and visitors from Rome, both Jews and proselytes, [11] Cretans and Arabians, we hear them telling in our own tongues the mighty works of God."

Antioch the Great

A series of kings named Antiochus founded cities and named them Antioch, but one of those Antiochs was Antioch the Great! It was the third largest city in the Roman Empire behind only Rome and Alexandria! It was home to half a million people in Paul's time. It is surely the biggest city of which we have never heard in the book of Acts. Unfortunately, Paul never wrote a letter to the Antiocheans like he did to the Corinthians. Had he done so we would have known about this great metropolis. Let me tell you a little about it.

Today, Antioch (Antakya) is in Turkey, but in the time of Paul it was in the Roman Province of Syria, just around the upper right hand corner of the Mediterranean from Tarsus and Cilicia. Antioch is 150 miles from Tarsus and 300 miles north of Jerusalem. These two cities were, in the time of Paul, the capitals of their respective provinces, Cilicia and Syria. Like Tarsus, Antioch was a few miles inland from the Mediterranean—fourteen to be exact. The river Orontes which flows through Antioch was navigable from the sea as far as Antioch in the first century giving the city a commercial link to all the ports around the Mediterranean. The actual port city for Antioch was Seleucia—a city from which Paul, Barnabas and John Mark set sail to go to Cyprus on their first missionary journey (Acts 13:4).

Like Damascus, Antioch was located at the foot of a

mountain, Mt. Silpius, and like Damascus a river, the Orontes, flowed through it. In Paul's time the Orontes bifurcated and formed an island on which part of the city was built. The city was framed by the mountain on its east and the river on its west. South of the city there was a famous suburb known as Daphne which had numerous springs and was the prime residential area. "Daphne was a picturesque garden spot, overlooking the Orontes. It was made fertile and beautiful by numerous natural springs, which not only provided an ample supply of water for the local villas, baths and gardens, but furnished Antioch with a large part of its water, conducted to the city through aqueducts which skirt the lower slopes of the mountain."[41] Daphne has been excavated and has yielded magnificent floor mosaics from the sumptuous houses there. Most of the mosaics come from after Paul's lifetime but they indicate the relative wealth and splendor of that area in the first century. The floor plan and some of the mosaics of a public bath house on the island in Antioch have been uncovered, and this structure does date to the first century, so Paul may very well have used the facility.

After capturing Cilicia and Syria and much of Mesopotamia, Alexander the Great died in 323 B.C., and one of his generals became the king over this region—the whole eastern end of the Roman Empire. It is hard for us to imagine the im-

---

[41] Glanville Downey, *Ancient Antioch* (Princeton, NJ: Princeton University Press, 1963) 15.

pact the Greeks had on the lands they conquered. The Greek language, their educational system, their architecture, their sculpture and art and their religions all captured the hearts and minds of the people they conquered. Nowhere was this more true than in the region at the eastern end of the Mediterranean—the so-called Seleucid Empire. Antioch became the capital of this empire and the Greek way of life was built into the city from its very founding. This had a profound effect on the Jews in Israel because these Seleucids ruled Israel for many years and tried to force the Jews to live as Greeks. The Greek origins and culture of Antioch also had a profound effect on the Christian church which developed there as we shall see.

Antioch and Jews

The Jewish historian, Josephus said that Jews were

"particularly numerous in Syria, where intermingling is due to the proximity of the two countries. But it was at Antioch that they specially congregated, partly owing to the greatness of that city, but mainly because the successors of King Antiochus had enabled them to live there in security. For, although Antiochus surnamed Epiphanes sacked Jerusalem and plundered the temple, his successors on the throne restored to the Jews of Antioch all such votive offerings as were made of brass, to be laid up in their synagogue, and, moreover, granted them citizen rights on an equality with the Greeks. Continuing to receive similar treatment from later monarchs, the Jewish colony grew in numbers, and their richly designed and costly offerings formed a splendid ornament to the temple. Moreover, they were constantly attracting to their religious ceremonies multitudes of Greeks, and these they had in some measure incorporated with themselves."[42]

The fact that there were Jews in the Seleucid capital seems odd to those whose only knowledge of the Seleucid empire comes from the Old Testament. The book of Daniel depicts the atrocities of the second century B.C. Seleucid king, Antiochus IV Epiphanes, in gruesome detail. In the Apocrypha, the books of the Maccabees give even greater detail in this regard. It is hard to imagine Jews living in the capital city of the man who had a pig slaughtered on the altar in Jerusalem and plundered the Temple there. Apparently, however, apart from the reign of Antiochus IV, Jews fared well in Antioch under Seleucid rule and there were a lot of them who lived there. Population figures are not precise by any means but even in the first century Jews in Antioch numbered in the tens of thou-

---

[42] Josephus, *Wars of the Jews,*. 7.44-45, trans. H. St. J. Thackeray in *Josephus with an English Translation* 3 (LCL; Cambridge, MA: Harvard; London: Heinemann, 1961).

sands. They were self governing under the leadership of a "ruler" who presided over a council of "elders."[43]

One feature of Jewish life in Antioch may have been part of the "fullness of time" that made it possible for the Gospel to spread across the Roman world. In the quotation from Josephus used above the Jewish historian noted that the Jews in Antioch "were constantly attracting to their religious ceremonies multitudes of Greeks, and these they had in some measure incorporated with themselves." Everywhere there was Judaism there were non-Jews who became "god-fearers" and were closely related to the synagogues. They were somewhat like those who are "watchcare" members in a Baptist church. At Antioch, however, this process was much more robust than elsewhere, and this doubtless played a major role in the open-

---

[43] Raymond E. Brown and John Meier, *Antioch and Rome* (New York: Paulist Press,1983) 31: "The Jewish community at Antioch seems to have been presided over by some chief officer, whom Josephus calls the "ruler" *(archon)* of the Antiochene Jews." Meeks-Wilken suggest that he was the head of the council of elders *(gerousiarchos)*. The elders, in turn, were the representatives of the various synagogues in the city and in the suburb of Daphne. The council of elders *(gerousia)* would thus be the governing body for all Antiochene Jews.[74] One wonders whether the structure of one ruler presiding over a body of elders might have provided a remote model for the one bishop *(episkopos)* presiding over a council of elders *(presbyterion* in Christian Antioch at the time of Ignatius."

ness to Gentile Christians at Antioch—the first place we know of where Gentiles were fully incorporated into the church.

Antioch and Christians

The Book of Acts (11:19-20) tells us how Christians came to be in Antioch:

> Now those scattered on account of the persecution which broke out because of Stephen journeyed as far as Phoenicia, Cyprus, and Antioch, speaking the [Christian] message to no one except Jews. But there were some of them, men from Cyprus and Cyrene, who, when they came to Antioch, spoke [the Christian message] to Gentiles as well, proclaiming [to them] the good news of the Lord Jesus.

Stephen was martyred soon after Jesus' crucifixion, possibly in 32 A.D. Soon after that some—perhaps many—Christians left Jerusalem, especially those like Stephen who were Greek speaking Jews who were not natives of Israel. Some went to other cities in Israel like Caesarea where Simon Peter later encountered Cornelius, but others left Israel and went north to Phoenicia, the island of Cyprus and the city of Antioch. Acts tells us explicitly that these scattered Christians witnessed only to Jews everywhere except in Antioch. In Antioch the witnesses whose birthplaces were outside Israel—the island of Cyprus and the coast of North Africa (Cyrene)—took the message to non-Jews-- Gentiles. Jewish

Christians with Greek backgrounds took the message to Gentiles whose culture was Greek. We may know the names of some of these early witnesses who were Hellenists (Greek speaking Jews): Lucius of Cyrene and Symeon Niger (13:1) were members of the church in Antioch. It is interesting that one of the seven Hellenists "deacons" was Nicolaus, a Gentile from Antioch who had become a Jewish convert (6:5).[44] He may have been one who went back to Antioch.

Thus it would appear that the nucleus of Christians who made up the church in Antioch were Hellenists—Jews who came from outside Israel--the diaspora[45]--and spoke Greek.

---

[44] It is just possible that Barnabas, himself "a Cypriot (4:36), could have been among the scattered Cypriot and Cyrenean Hellenists who began the Gentile mission at Antioch." See Brown and Meier, 33. Meier goes on to note (p. 35) that "The next reliable piece of information[83] is the list of "prophets and teachers" at Antioch in Acts 13:1.[84] The five named are Barnabas (note his position at the head of the list), Lucius of Cyrene, Manaen (Menahem), who was a childhood companion of the tetrarch Herod Antipas, and Saul (placed at the end). That a childhood companion *(syntrophos)* of Herod should be a leader in the early days of the Antiochene church serves as a reminder that Christianity did not start out as a "slave" religion and did not entirely lack members from the higher strata of society."

[45] "In the first century some five to six million Jews were living in Diaspora, that is, more or less permanently settled outside Palestine. The Diaspora had begun at least as early as the deportations of the Babylonian exile, in the sixth century, and had been fed by subsequent dislocations through successive conquests of the homeland, but even more by voluntary emigration in search of better economic opportunities than the limited space and wealth of Palestine could afford. Consequently there was a substantial Jewish population in virtually every town of any size in the lands bordering the Mediterranean. Esti-

These are the ones who first heard the message on Pentecost in their own languages. Luke mentioned all the places from which they came in Acts 2. The city of Antioch with its Hellenistic origins and culture welcomed these Greek speaking Christians. When the church in Jerusalem heard about this extension of the Gospel to non-Jews they chose one of their own who came from outside Israel and spoke Greek to go investigate. They chose Barnabas, a diaspora Jew from Cyprus, who spoke Greek like the ones in Antioch, to represent them. And Luke tells us that Barnabas was "glad" at what he found in Antioch and this is where Paul comes in.

Antioch and Paul

If Tarsus gave us Saul, and Damascus gave us Paul, it was really Antioch that gave us the Apostle Paul, the missionary to Asia, Macedonia, Greece and Italy. After Paul's vision of Christ on the Damascus Road he spent time east of Damascus in Arabia or what was then called Nabataea. Perhaps it was not safe for this zealous Jew who had experienced a complete change in his zeal to remain in Damascus. He later returned to Damascus but soon left- not to go back to Jerusalem which would not have been safe for him either- but to go home to Tarsus. For some eight years Paul lived in Tarsus. We can only assume that he spent these years thinking about Christ, re-

---

mates run from 10 to 15 percent of the total population of a city—in the case of Alexandria, perhaps even higher." Meeks, *The First Urban Christians*, 34.

reading the Old Testament in the light of Christ's crucifixion and witnessing to all who would listen, though we know of no church he left behind in Tarsus.

Then one day, Barnabas, a Jew and a Christian whose home was on the island of Cyprus came to get him. The rest as they say is history. Obviously when Barnabas saw the make-up of the congregation in Antioch he thought of another diaspora Jewish Christian who could lead this congregation. We don't know whether there had been contact between Paul and Barnabas over the intervening years or not but Barnabas had not forgotten Paul. Apparently Paul came to mind because he had already presented the Gospel to Gentiles himself and could minister to Gentiles in the fellowship at Antioch. Luke tells us that Barnabas and Paul "met with the church, and taught a large company of people" for a whole year "and in Antioch the disciples were for the first time called Christians" (Acts 11:25).[46] The fact that a new name, distinct from the name "Jew," was given this group indicates that the group was large enough to

---

[46] "*Christianoi,* "followers or supporters of Christ," is best explained as a Latin title given to the disciples by Gentiles, perhaps the Roman authorities, who took *Christus* to be a proper name, not a title. The very fact of a special name indicates that the Gentiles perceived the Christians to be something more than merely a group of Jews, no doubt because of the Gentiles admitted to full membership without circumcision or full observance of the Mosaic Law." Brown and Meier, 35, footnote 81.

65

come to the attention of the government in Antioch. They were a separate and distinct group though obviously closely related to Jews.

The church in Antioch became Paul's home church. He, along with others, was the minister there (Luke calls them "prophets and teachers."). The year he spent teaching in Antioch surely was foundational for his theology although much of this was doubtless shaped over the eight previous years in Tarsus.[47] Here he applied the Gospel.

This was the church that ordained him for missions. Luke says that

> "While they were worshipping the Lord and fasting, the Holy Spirit said, 'Set apart for me Barnabas and Saul for the work to which I have called them.' Then after fasting and praying they laid their hands on them and sent them off." (Acts 13:2-3)

It was a moment comparable to the ordination of the first deacons (Acts 6:1-6) with ultimate ramifications that could hardly have been foreseen by those involved. This was the church that sent Paul some ten thousand miles on foot across the Roman Empire. It was the church that placed his life in danger from

---

[47] See Martin Hengel, *Paul Between Damascus and Antioch* (Louisville: Westminster John Knox,1997) 11-14 for the importance of these early years in the development of Paul's theology.

imprisonments, beatings, stoning, shipwreck, and the 'false brethren.'

This was the church to which he returned after each mission with a report of what God had done through his work.

And, as sometimes is the case, this was the church that broke his heart! Here he experienced the heartbreak and pain of broken relationships. Paul himself tells the story in Galatians 2. After the first missionary journey to Cyprus and Galatia some in Jerusalem had demanded that Paul require circumcision of all Gentiles wishing to be Christians—that is that like Jews they had to keep the law. Paul and Barnabas went to Jerusalem and hammered out an agreement with James and Peter that did not require circumcision for non-Jews and that story is told in Acts 15. Some time after that agreement was reached, however, representatives from the Jerusalem church went to Paul's converts in Galatia and demanded that they obey the law, and they apparently accepted this demand. Paul wrote a letter addressing them as "foolish Galatians" and angrily upbraiding them for abandoning the Gospel of grace which he preached. In this letter he told of an episode in Antioch that was very painful. Peter had come for a visit to Antioch and had fellowshipped with the Hellenist Christians there, some of whom were Gentiles. He had been willing to eat with them publicly. And then the ultra conservatives from Jerusalem arrived and Peter no longer would eat at the same table as the

Gentiles. Paul says he "withstood him to his face" (Acts 2:11). Even more painful to Paul, Barnabas his friend, mentor, and fellow missionary sided with Peter. Paul felt abandoned. This episode apparently was part of the reason Paul and Barnabas went separately on the next mission. Barnabas took Mark and went back to his home island of Cyprus. Paul took Silas and returned to Galatia and beyond. Paul does not mention a broken heart in his list of sufferings, but the controversy over circumcision must have left deep scars.

Paul's second journey ended with a visit to the church in Jerusalem[48] and then a return to Antioch. He had left Antioch three years earlier obviously disturbed by the controversy with Peter and Barnabas. Neither Luke nor Paul himself tells us what it was like to return to his home church. Luke simply says that he "went down to Antioch" and "After spending some time there he departed" and began his third trip across the Roman province of Galatia and Asia—a trip that would end up in Jerusalem and result in imprisonment ultimately in Rome. One can't help wondering what it was like to return to Antioch after such an intense disagreement with Barnabas and Peter. Luke does not tell us whether Barnabas had returned from his mission trip to Cyprus and we don't know where Simon Peter was at this point.

---

[48] Luke says "When he had landed at Caesarea, he went up and greeted the church…" This clearly means that he went up to Jerusalem though Luke makes nothing of this visit. Acts 18:22

Conclusion

Surely Paul's invitation to Antioch was every bit as significant as his later call from Macedonia to "come over and help us." He was instrumental in establishing the First Church of Antioch, the church in the great metropolis of the middle east. It was this great church that gave us "Christians" because it was here that Christians and Jews began to be different enough to require separate labels. It was this great church that gave us "missionaries" for it was this church's decision to send some of its own with the Gospel to the rest of the Empire that began the noble enterprise of Christian missions. And, in a very real sense, it was this great church that gave us denominations for it was here that the first painful division between Christians over theological issues occurred. Had Paul not stood his ground, the history of Christianity would have been vastly different. May we always disagree only over things that really matter.

Chapter 5

The Cities That Gave Us "Galatians"

If Paul wrote letters to the churches of Tarsus, Damascus and Antioch in Syria, we don't any longer have copies of them. When Paul wrote a letter to a church and that letter has been preserved in our Bible, the name of the city involved has become a household word known the world over. In this chapter we finally are dealing with cities to which Paul did write—but the letter he wrote was perhaps a circular letter to several churches in one geographical region and the names of the churches have not been included in the letter. To make matters worse, scholars have debated for years the location of the churches to which the letter was sent! We now think we know which churches are involved, but some still debate the matter. How's that for getting no respect!

The context for this study is Paul's first missionary journey which took him and his companions, Barnabas and John Mark, from their home church in Antioch (in Syria) to the island of Cyprus (where Barnabas was born) and on to what we know of today as Turkey. After sailing from Syria to Cyprus, the group walked some one hundred miles all the way across the southern side of Cyprus from Salamis (Famagusta today) to Paphos. Luke does not mention the several cities the group would have walked through on their way to Paphos, perhaps because they did not have success in those cities. Their time in Paphos was much more productive, however, because it was there that a high Roman official, one Lucius Sergius Paulus, accepted Paul's message and became a Christian. This was Paul's Cornelius! Leaving Paphos by ship, the group landed on the southern shore of Turkey and moved inland a few miles to Perga. The only thing Luke tells us about what happened in Perga is that John Mark left the group and went back to Jerusalem. We are not told why but it may well have been that Mark was uncomfortable in the predominantly Gentile territory of Pamphylia. This would help explain why Paul did not want to take him on his second trip.

Following the group's arrival in the region of Pamphylia, Luke says that the group "passed on from Perga and came to Antioch of Pisidia" (Acts 13:14). The road north from Perga to Antioch passes through the Taurus Mountains and was known to be a dangerous route both because of natural hazards and because of human bandits. Paul himself may have referred to this road in 2 Corinthians ll:26-27 when he says that he was frequently "in danger from rivers, danger from robbers, …danger in the wilderness…through many a sleepless night, in hunger and thirst, often without food, in cold and exposure." The road ascends over the mountains through a snow covered pass to the high plains of central Turkey.

Luke goes on to tell us about four cities in which Paul preached: Antioch in Pisidia, Iconium, Lystra and Derbe. Apparently these are the cities that gave us the letter to the Galatians. I say "apparently" because these are the only cities in the region in which we know that Paul preached. The uncertainty over identifying these four cities as cities of Galatia comes from their location. It was once thought that the province of Galatia was further north, but it is clear now that these four cities were all within the territory known as Galatia at the time. Sir William Ramsay made the case for the location of all these cities in Galatia more than a century ago. It was he who pointed out that within the Roman province of Galatia there were distinct regions: Phrygia, Isauria, Pisidia, and Lycaonia. [49] Preaching in these cities nearly cost Paul his life but his famous letter to the Christians in Galatia is his signature defense of faith in Christ as the key to salvation. It was this letter along with Romans that gave us the Reformation and remains to this day as the classic assertion of the primacy of faith. Since he did not single out any one of his churches in Galatia to receive the letter, we need to look briefly at them all.

Antioch in Pisidia

The ruins of Pisidian Antioch lie about a mile north of the modern town of Yalvaç, which is 110 miles west of Konya (Iconium) and 125 miles north of Perga where Paul and Barnabas began their walk.

It just may be that the proconsul on Cyprus who accepted Paul's preaching had something to do with the choice of Antioch in Pisidia as the place to preach Christ. A stone inscription has been found by archaeologists noting the name of one Lucius Sergius Paulus the Younger who was a significant figure in Antioch. It is just possible that this is the son of the man to whom Paul witnessed on Cyprus, but if it is we have no

---

[49] William M. Ramsay, *St Paul the Traveller and The Roman Citizen* (Grand Rapids: Baker Book House, 1960 [reprinted from 1897]), 104.

indication that he heard Paul receptively or that he helped Paul when the crowds of Antioch turned against him.

Antioch was a major city with all the features prominent in such cities, baths, paved colonnaded streets, stadium, nymphaeum [fountain], aqueduct, and temples. There were Roman roads in the area, and Antioch was on one of them, an important new highway (the Via Sebaste, constructed in 6 BC) that connected the interior of Asia Minor with the coast. "There were two main streets in the city, the Decumanus Maximus (the main east-west road) and the Cardo Maximus (the north-south road) , the remains of which are still visible today. "The Cardo terminated at the 1st-century AD nymphaeum, a fountain from which water was distributed to the whole city. Behind it, a 1st-century aqueduct brought water down from the hills to the city. To the northwest of the nymphaeum is the palaestra (exercise area) and adjoining Roman bath. A large part of the bathhouse has survived and is still being excavated. "[50]

The main square of the city was the Augusta Platea which had a triumphal gateway composed of three arches. On the square sat the great temple of Augustus celebrating the victories of the emperor. In earlier times temples to other gods and goddesses had graced the square. It must have been an imposing sight but it apparently did not intimidate Paul and Barnabas.

---

[50] http://www.sacred-destinations.com/turkey/pisidian-antioch

On the west side of the Cardo Maximus, are the remains of a Byzantine church dating from the 4th or 5th century AD. A century ago some foundations protruding from beneath the Byzantine church were discovered and although it cannot be proved, some believe they are the foundations of a 1st-century synagogue. If so, it would be one of the few first-century synagogues found outside the Holy Land. It would also mean that the pilgrim can read Paul's sermon in Acts 13 in the very place it was delivered.

In Luke's account there are only two Sabbaths mentioned but it seems likely that Paul and Barnabas witnessed in Antioch for some time. This was a large city with perhaps 100,000 residents and a large Jewish population. It would have taken some time for word to have reached a large number of these people so Luke may have telescoped events that took some time to develop. However, after Paul preached in the synagogue "devout women" and "leading men of the city" rallied the populace against Paul and Barnabas and they left Antioch. It isn't clear whether their departure was a hasty one to avoid physical harm or simply a departure after the protests of the citizens. Luke does not tell us how many people believed Paul's message, but he has a cryptic sentence which says that "as many as were ordained to eternal life believed" (Acts 13:48). He also mentioned that Paul's message spread beyond the city itself to the region of which Antioch was the capital.[51] It is clear that " the first thor-

---

[51] "There can be no doubt that Pisidian Antioch…was the centre of the *Region* called Phrygia.…This central importance of Antioch was due to its position as

oughly Gentile congregation separate from the synagogue was established at Pisidian Antioch."[52]

Iconium

When Paul and Barnabas left Antioch they travelled along the Via Sebaste, a new (in Paul's day) Roman road linking Ephesus on the west coast with Tarsus at the eastern end of Asia Minor. This road linked Antioch in Pisidia with Iconium and another city not mentioned in Acts, Laranda, in a roughly straight line. Iconium was some 110 miles from Antioch—about a week's walk. Ramsay compares the setting of Iconium nestled under a mountain to that of Damascus. Both cities had perennial water supplies and were thus very desirable locations and both were very ancient cities. Iconium was never so much at the center of events as was Damascus and thus was less famous. Today, Iconium is known as Konya and is a major city of over a million people in Turkey and the center of its region. "Jalal al-Din Rumi (c. 1207-73) a famous Muslim mystic and poet fled from Afghanistan and settled here. He became a mystic, or Sufi and his followers formed the Mevlevi order of dervishes, sometimes known in the West as the 'whirling dervishes,' after their dance that emulates the movement of planets on their journey of spir-

---

a Roman Colony, which made it the military and administrative centre of the country." Ramsay, 104

[52] Ramsay, 102

itual fulfillment."[53] Thus Paul and Barnabas have to share the religious spotlight in Iconium with a whirling dervish!

Luke tells us very little about what Paul and Barnabas did in Iconium. He says that they stayed there a "long time" and spoke to both Jews and Greeks. At some point both groups united against Paul and Barnabas and tried to stone them. Luke says Paul and Barnabas "fled" from Iconium, apparently indicating that they left hastily and escaped from a mob action against them. William Ramsay points out that the pair of evangelists were ordered out of Antioch by city officials who had been influenced by "ladies of high rank who were within the influence of the Synagogue." However, at Iconium they were confronted not by legal authorities but by a mob which tried to harm them.[54] Luke gave us no details about how their departure from Iconium was accomplished, but this time they not only left town but they left the region.

Lystra

Lystra was eighteen miles from Iconium. Today it is called Klistra and there are few visible reminders of the events that took place there about the year 50 A.D. Lystra has not been excavated. When Paul and Barnabas left Iconium and came to Lystra they moved into a different district within Galatia called

---

[53] http://www.pbs.org/empires/islam/profilesrumi.html

[54] Ramsay, 371.

76

Lycaonia.[55] Luke tells us that the people there spoke Lycaonian and identified Paul and Barnabas with gods that were worshipped there. Ramsay points out that it was here that Paul "is brought into immediate contact with the uneducated Anatolian populace, ignorant of Hellenic culture, speaking the Lycaonian tongue…"[56] Luke does not mention how many people were convinced by Paul and Barnabas but he mentions "disciples" (Acts 14:21) of Paul. Whether these were travelling with him or those whom he had just met we do not know. It is interesting that when Paul returned to Lystra on a subsequent journey, he met a young man who had a Jewish mother ("who was a believer" [Acts 16:1]) and a pagan father. His name was "Timothy," and Timothy is called a "disciple." Timothy was well known to Christians in both Lystra and Iconium so obviously Paul had succeeded in convincing some people in both cities that Jesus was the Christ crucified for them.

Lystra is best known for the flip-flop by the people there from excited adulation to angry rejection. After Paul had succeeded in helping a crippled man walk, the people along with the priest of the temple of Zeus tried to offer a sacrifice of thanksgiving to Paul and Barnabas. They had identified the older, more mature Barnabas with their chief god, Zeus, and Paul, the preacher with the messenger god, Hermes. Paul and Barnabas

---

[55] William M. Ramsay, *St Paul the Traveller and the Roman Citizen* (Grand Rapids: Baker Book House, 1960 [reprint from 1897]), 110.

[56] Ramsay, *Cities*, 409

refused the adulation and preached to them a general message urging them to leave their traditional worship and turn to "the living God." Paul did not preach about Christ crucified, perhaps because these lesser educated people had not had the background afforded by contact with Jews. There is no synagogue mentioned in Lystra. "Perhaps for the first time in his missionary work, Paul was reaching Gentiles with the gospel of Christ without approaching them through the common ground of Judaism."[57]

After this episode Luke says that people came from the cities in which Paul had already preached, Antioch and Iconium, and persuaded the people to stone Paul which they did, leaving him for dead outside the city limits. Either this stoning was not as severe as the one that killed Stephen or there was a miraculous deliverance of Paul. Luke says Paul not only "rose up" but was able to walk away from Lystra the next day! This would not normally have been possible for anyone hit with heavy stones. Paul never forgot this experience! He reminded his Corinthian readers of it when he listed all that he had endured for Christ's sake: "once I was stoned" (2 Corinthians 11:25).

Derbe

On the first missionary journey, Derbe gets just part of two sentences. After Paul was stoned by the crowd at Lystra, Luke writes that "on the next day he [Paul] went with Barnabas to Derbe. When they had preached the gospel to that city and

---

[57] http://en.wikipedia.org/wiki/Lystra

had made many disciples, they returned to Lystra and to Iconium and to Antioch [in Pisidia] strengthening the souls of the disciples, exhorting them to continue in the faith ..." (Acts 14:20-21).

Derbe had little to commend it to a person like Paul whose mode of operation was to go to the great urban centers, but it was safely away from Lystra where he had nearly been killed. The most likely site of Derbe lies about 15 miles (24 km) north northeast of the city of Karaman, Turkey (ancient Laranda) on a mound known as Kerti Hüyük. Laranda was the major city in the area and the Imperial Highway that passed through Derbe was intended to provide a link between Laranda and Antioch in Pisidia. Why Paul did not press on to Laranda we do not know.

The Return to Antioch in Syria

To those of us who read the book of Acts it must appear remarkable that Paul could turn around and go back through three towns in which he had been stoned, run out of town by a mob and ejected by the police. Apparently in all of these towns Paul had won the hearts of some of the population and they helped him on the journey back. It would have been possible for Paul and Barnabas to continue eastward through the Cilician Gates to Tarsus and then overland to Antioch in Syria, depending on the time of year which we are not told. If winter were approaching it would have been impossible to go through the high mountains to Tarsus.

Paul and Barnabas decided to go back the way they came

visiting Lystra, Iconium and Antioch again. In each city they must have taught and encouraged those who had believed. Luke says that Paul appointed "elders" in every church. This was the common practice later but one wonders whether the small groups of Christians in each city were large enough for any kind of hierarchy to be needed.

On the return home Paul and Barnabas once again went south to Perga and this time they preached in the city. We are given no information about their success. It was just a short walk of a few miles to Attalia on the Mediterranean where they took passage on a boat going to Seleucia, the port that served Antioch in Syria.

What Did These Four Cities Give Us

If Tarsus gave us Saul, and Damascus gave us Paul, and Antioch in Syria gave us christians, what did the cities of Galatia leave as their legacy? It was their honor to be the first places where Paul presented his gospel to pure Gentiles—in one case in a town that did not even have a synagogue. It was to them that Paul preached his message of Christ crucified as the fulfillment of the Old Testament prophecies of the Messiah. It was to them, Jew and Gentile alike, that Paul argued that the law had done all it could for us by bringing us to Christ. Once God had acted in Christ, Paul reasoned that keeping the law would not help. Just accept what God has done on behalf of sinners and experience the indwelling spirit of God. And it was to these four churches

that Paul wrote his famous letter we know of as Galatians. This
is the legacy they gave us. It is Paul's famous manifesto of freedom from the law. In some ways it is Paul's autobiography. It is
in this letter that Paul affirmed:

> I have been crucified with Christ; it is no longer I
> who live but Christ who lives in me; and the life I
> now live in the flesh I live by faith in the son of
> God, who loved me and gave himself for me.
> (Gal 2:20).

Chapter 6

Troas: The City That Gave Us A Vision

Troas was Paul's third choice of places to work! Luke tells us in Acts 16 that Paul and Silas picked up Timothy at Lystra on Paul's second missionary journey and headed west into territory that was new to Paul. Paul wanted to enter the Roman province of Asia but he was "forbidden by the Holy Spirit to speak the word in Asia" (Acts 16:6). Then he "attempted to go [north] into Bithynia, but the Spirit of Jesus did not allow them" (Acts 16:7). Straight ahead was the only option, so Paul and his group went west to Troas. Thus it was that Paul received his famous vision to "come over to Macedonia and help us" because his original plans didn't work out. Talk about making lemonade when life hands you lemons and you've got the prime case right here.

Luke doesn't record any preaching by Paul in Troas on this trip but when he got back to Troas on his third journey there was a church there. This is the place where Paul spoke at length and a boy named Eutychus went to sleep and fell out of an upper story window (Acts 20:7-12). Apparently Paul had found some persons there who had become believers on his first visit. There is no letter to the church at Troas in our Bible so it receives very little recognition. This city deserves our study though in more ways than one. As we shall see, it was a major city in its own right and whatever happened there on the first missionary journey turned Paul to the west, and thereby hangs a tale. Others had already taken the gospel to Rome, so perhaps the west would have been touched by the Christian faith without Paul's preaching, but the churches that came into being as a result of Paul's vision at Troas shaped much of our early theology.

Let's start back with the time when Paul left the region of Galatia on this second journey and see if we can trace his route to Troas. We need to look briefly at the places Paul was forbidden to go. Then we will explore Troas itself, its significance within the Roman Empire and the role it played in Paul's ministry.

The Places He Didn't Go (And Why He Didn't Go There)

One look at different maps of the Roman provinces tells us that the lines are not drawn with a great deal of precision on the maps of Asia Minor in our Bibles! The regions of Phrygia and Galatia through which Paul and his companions walked vary in location by a hundred miles or more on these maps. And Luke does not name a single city or recognizable place between Lystra in the middle of modern Turkey and the coast of the Aegean Sea, a distance of some 300 miles as the crow flies and many more by the roads. Thus scholars are reduced to reasoning which route Paul would have taken based on the known roads in the region at the time.[58] The region is mountainous and people on foot would have necessarily taken the roads in the valleys when these were available, but even with this much help Paul's route has not been obvious.[59] There is a major scholarly effort underway to fill in this gap in our knowledge, but it may be years coming to fruition.[60]

While we can't know exactly which route Paul followed, we know of two regions in which he did not do missionary work: Asia and Bithynia. The "Asia" in which Paul did not work isn't the "Asia" we think of when we hear that word. We think of the far eastern Orient, perhaps China. The "Asia" mentioned here is

---

[58] " Even the most recent, critical study Bible traces the route to Troas with a vague line, disregarding the few roads that have been identified, while arbitrarily crossing mountains and rivers as if Paul traveled by heliocopter." Robert Jewett, "Mapping The Route Of Paul's Second Missionary Journey From Dorylaeum To Troas" *Tyndale Bulletin 48.1 (1997).*

[59] David H. French indicates the need for further research in "Acts and the Roman Roads of Asia Minor," in D. W. J. Gill and C. Gempf, eds., *The Book of Acts in Its First Century Setting.* Vol. 2. *The Book of Acts in Its Graeco-Roman Setting* (Grand Rapids: Eerdmans; Carlisle: Paternoster, 1994) 49-58, which concludes (56) that with regard to the 2nd missionary journey, "The roads and routes taken by Paul cannot be established and, accordingly, there is not as yet a demonstrable correlation between his journeys and the then existing Romans Roads." He suggests that the routes through Galatia were on unpaved roads.

[60] The project was presented to the scholarly world in a 2005 lecture by Robert Jewett, Guest Professor of New Testament, University of Heidelberg entitled " The Troas Project: Investigating Maritime And Land Routes To Clarify The Role Of Alexandria Troas In Commerce And Religion," An Illustrated Lecture for the 2005 CSBS Seminar (29-31 May 2005) .

the western part of modern day Turkey, the Roman province of Asia. It is the area to which John wrote his letters in the book of Revelation, the letters to "the seven churches of Asia." It is the heavily populated Aegean coastal region with its famous city of Ephesus and many other major centers of population. Paul had apparently set his heart on taking the gospel to this populous Greek speaking area of the Empire, but Luke says mysteriously that Paul was "forbidden by the Holy Spirit to speak the word in Asia." Luke does not say that Paul was forbidden to enter the province of Asia. Indeed it would have been difficult to get to Troas without going through Asia. Luke said that Paul was forbidden to "speak the word in Asia." Apparently he felt compelled not to do missionary work in the region toward which he was originally pointed. We can hardly keep from wondering what prohibited him from witnessing there. Was it a matter of territorial claim? Did another apostle or missionary have the church's blessing to take the good news to Asia? Was there danger that way for Paul? Luke attributes the hindrance to God's will, noting that the "Holy Spirit" forbade Paul. Whether the Holy Spirit spoke through a Christian prophet or some sign we do not know. We know from a later episode in Acts (21:7-14) that a Christian prophet urged Paul not to go to Jerusalem saying, "Thus says the Holy Spirit, So shall the Jews at Jerusalem bind the man who owns this girdle.... ." Whatever the circumstances, Ephesus would have to wait for Paul!

The other area in which Paul did not work was Bithynia.

This area is much less familiar than the Roman province of Asia, many of whose cities we know. Bithynia was north and east of the province of Asia. Bithynia began just east of what is today Istanbul and, along with the province of Pontus, formed the southern shore of the Black Sea. Not a single city in Bithynia is mentioned in our New Testament, but the cities of Chalcedon and Nicea which lie in this region were the hosts for major councils of the early church. From the latter council we get the Nicene Creed which some churches use instead of the Apostles' Creed. While no cities are named in the letter, I Peter is addressed to the "exiles of the Dispersion" (I Peter 1:1) in the provinces of Bithynia and Pontus. Outside the New Testament there is a famous letter from a Governor of Bithynia, a man named Pliny, to the Emperor Trajan asking for advice on how to deal with Christians brought before his court.[61] Clearly someone took the gospel to Bithynia very early, and there were many who professed Christ even unto death by the year 112 A.D., but it was not Paul because he was forbidden "by the Spirit of Jesus" to go into Bithynia. Again we have no clue as to why Paul was prevented from going north to Bithynia.

---

[61] Pliny says it was his custom to ask people accused if they were Christians and have them offer incense to the emperor's statue and "revile" the name of Jesus "none of which things, I understand, any genuine Christian can be induced to do" (Correspondence With the Emperor Trajan, 10.96.5 [Loeb Classical Library]).

Why Troas?

Paul couldn't go north or south. His only choices apparently were to return back through Phrygia and Galatia where he had previously established churches or to go straight ahead. He had already made three trips through Galatia, two on the first missionary journey and a third on his way to this point on the second missionary journey. Understandably then, Paul chose to go forward. Luke says they came to a decision point as they approached the province of Mysia. The scholar who is heading up the Troas Project mentioned above concludes that "Dorylaeum is the point opposite Mysia which has a major highway leading north into Bithynia.... Dorylaeum was the location where the decision not to go into Bithynia was made"[62] From this point on Paul "must either have aimed at Adramyttium on the seacoast where the coastal highway ...led to Troas; or ...[have gone] overland on roads unknown to modern researchers through the Aisepos and Scamander valleys and down into Troas. The expression 'they descended into Troas', would accurately describe a journey down into the coastal city from the mountainous country to the east of Troas.[63] The route suggested by this scholar would have taken Paul through ten small Roman towns and several mining centers in the district of Mysia. Since the district of Mysia was part of the province of Asia, the injunction against preaching in Asia must have kept Paul from preaching in any of

---

[62] Jewett, *op.cit*, 5

[63] Jewett, *op.cit*, 6

these population centers. Of course, these towns may not have had Jewish synagogues and, thus, may not have afforded Paul an opening to discuss the gospel with the people. We may never know why Paul was not able to establish churches all across Mysia as he did in Galatia. Perhaps he simply wanted to spend his energy in the big city of Troas on the sea coast rather than in the smaller inland cities. Troas itself, however, was in Asia and apparently Paul did not feel free to witness there either on this first visit. On his next trip to the region—the third missionary journey—Paul tells us in 2 Corinthians 2:12-13 that "a door was opened for me in the Lord" and "I came to Troas to preach the gospel of Christ." Years after the first visit to Troas Paul finally got to preach the gospel there and apparently established the church there. He returned to Troas some months later and preached again. This time he spoke at night and Luke tells us that a boy went to sleep and fell out of an upper story window.[64] On one of these trips or a subsequent one that neither Luke nor Paul mentions Paul left some books, parchments and a cloak with a man named Carpus who lived in Troas. Paul asked Timothy to bring these items to him when he came (2 Timothy 4:13).

Troas is not well known to most Bible readers, but it was one of the most significant cities of all the Roman empire.[65] The excavation of Troas has been ongoing since 1993 by an archeological

---

[64]Acts 20:7-12

[65] A YouTube video which shows the road Paul walked and both Troas and nearby Troy is available at: http://www.youtube.com/watch?v=0hGUsaHeExM&noredirect=1

team from the University of Münster and the major components of the city have been uncovered.[66] Troas was a large city for its time. It was more than 1000 acres in size, with a very large population estimated to be somewhere between 50,000 and 100,000 people. "It had an artificial harbor… and was so strategically important as a transportation and administrative center that it was seriously considered by Julius Caesar as a potential site for the capital of the empire."[67] The harbor at Troas was important because ships needing to go through the narrow passages to the Black Sea needed a safe anchoring site while they waited for the right time to attempt the trip north. But even more important for our story, ships making the short crossing of the Aegean Sea west to Neapolis and Philippi in Macedonia started their journey from Troas. This was a primary route for travelers on their way to and from Rome. Thus Troas was a major hub for travelers—the Atlanta of its day—as well as a major administrative center for the Roman government. Whether Paul intended Troas as his goal after failing to be allowed to preach in Asia and Bithynia or whether he simply reached the sea coast and then had to decide how to proceed we do not know. Luke tells us of only one event in Troas—but it turned out to be a big event!

What About the Vision?

If Tarsus gave us Saul and Damascus gave us Paul, Troas gave us a vision that brought into sharp focus what God wanted

---

[66] See A. H. Cadwallader, *Stones, Bones, and the Sacred* (SBL Press, 2016) 273.

[67] Jewett, *op.cit*, 16-17

Paul to do. He arrived in Troas by default after failing to work in Asia and Bithynia. Luke doesn't tell us how long Paul stayed in Troas trying to decide what to do, but he does describe in unforgettable words what happened as Paul struggled with his decision:

> "And a vision appeared to Paul in the night: a man of Macedonia was standing beseeching him and saying, 'Come over to Macedonia and help us.'"

Luke has a way of telling us less than we want to know. He did it again here. He tells us that Paul saw a man from the Roman province of Macedonia across the Aegean from Troas in a vision. We aren't told how Paul knew he was a Macedonian. Macedonians would not have looked any different than the people of Troas. Apparently Paul had been weighing in his own mind whether to turn around and go back the way he had come or cross over to Macedonia. In the vision he saw a man from Macedonia calling to him. While many interpreters are consumed by the question of who the man from Macedonia was—many suggest that the man was none other than Luke for reasons we shall see in a moment—it is just as fascinating for me to ask what the man wanted from Paul. Was he a Christian who wanted Paul to help him preach? Was there already a tiny core of Christian believers in Philippi who needed to be strengthened? Or did Paul hear a lost world calling for help in finding a savior? I wonder if Paul saw this Macedonian as a Jew who needed help in understanding the scriptures about the Messiah. Or did Paul view him as a Gentile? As usual we can't answer these kinds of questions, but our image of the scene will inevitably affect our understanding of the event. The word "help" in this case usually refers to the need for protection or relief rather than the need for assistance, so Paul probably wasn't being summoned to assist others in preaching. The Macedonians seemed to be in need of Christ. While it has been customary in modern interpretations of this passage to emphasize the transition from Asia to Europe, no such emphasis is really involved. Macedonia, like Asia, was simply a province of the Roman Empire. It was not recognized as part of a different continent; rather it was part of the same empire, and it was this whole empire that Paul saw beckoning him across the Aegean

The next verse in Luke's account tells us that "when he had seen the vision, immediately we sought to go on into Macedonia, concluding that God had called us to preach the gospel to them" (Acts 16:10). This is the first of several "we" passages in Acts in which the author seems to include himself as part of Paul's group. For the first time in the book of Acts Luke writes with apparent first-hand knowledge of the events. He was no longer a historian; now he was an eye witness of the events unfolding. Again Luke has told us less than we want to know. Was it a chance meeting that brought Paul and Luke together or was this a rendezvous that had been planned? Had Luke just come across the Aegean from Macedonia or did he live in Troas? Already at this point Luke noted that the whole group concluded "that God had called us to preach the gospel to them (the Macedonians)." He included himself as one called to preach so he doe not seem to be a new Christian. When and where, then, did Luke become a Christian? The mysterious "we" passages seem to suggest that Luke joined Paul's group in Troas and was involved in the decision to cross the Aegean with the gospel. Since there is no indication that Luke lived in Troas, it seems reasonable to conclude that he had come from Macedonia perhaps with the intent of meeting Paul and perhaps bringing an encouragement to "come over to Macedonia to help us."

Conclusion

Ephesus, Colossae and the other cities of the Meander Valley would have to wait their turn to meet Paul. Bithynia with its teeming populations along the Black Sea would have to depend on another witness to the gospel. Paul was on a fast track to Troas and could not turn aside either North or South. A man named Luke suddenly appeared and with him a new vision of missionary fields on the other side of the Aegean. Macedonia may not have impressed Paul as being part of a new continent but it certainly did impress him as a new opportunity. It surely was no accident that Paul arrived at the one point on the whole Aegean coastline where it was normal and customary to board a ship for the west. A vision in the night at Troas was not unlike the famous flapping of butterfly wings in China that created a hurricane on the other side of the world.[68]

---

[68] In chaos theory, the butterfly effect is the sensitive dependence on initial conditions where a small change at one place in a nonlinear system can result in large differences to a later state." Ian Malcolm, the fictional scientist in both the novel and the movie, Jurassic Park, used it to explain the inherent instability of (among other things) an amusement park with dinosaurs as the attraction. For more on the "butterfly effect" see http://en.wikipedia.org/wiki/Butterfly_effect_in_popular_culture.

Chapter 7

Philippi: The City That Gave Paul Joy

No other book in the New Testament uses the words "joy" and "rejoice" more per page than the book of Philippians. "Joy" is the theme of the letter and the remarkable thing about Paul's hymn of joy is that it was written from jail—not the jail in Philippi where he and Silas were beaten and imprisoned, but the jail in Rome where his life hung in the balance. Paul noted in the letter that he was "at the point of being poured out" and he did not know what the outcome of his trial would be. But even with such anxiety weighing on him he remembered the Philippians with joy. They had been his partners from the very beginning he said and, near the end of his life when he wrote his letter to them, he was once again thanking them for a gift from them brought by Epaphroditus. This church was special to Paul! It was this city that gave him joy through its Christians even though his first experiences there were very painful.

Luke tells us some of what happened in Philippi, but he tells us almost nothing about the city itself. We'll look at the location of the city, what it looked like, its history and people and the religious life of the city when Paul arrived. Then we can look at the events that transpired in Philippi: the first encounter with a Jewish lady named Lydia; a confrontation with a young woman who said more than she realized; the public beating of Paul and Silas by the magistrate, jail, earthquake, conversion of the jailer and departure from the city.

The City of Philippi

The History of the City

The valley in which Philippi nestled was the scene of one of the most famous battles in all of recorded history. In 44 B.C. two Roman senators, Cassius and Brutus, led a conspiracy of some 60 Roman senators to assassinate Julius Caesar which they succeeded in doing on March 15th of that year, the Ides of March. Following Caesar's assassination, it turned out that Caesar had named his grandnephew, Gaius Octavian, 18 years old at the time, as his sole heir. Octavian joined forces with the older Mark Antony to put down the rebel forces lead by Cassius and Brutus. The two armies met on the plain outside Philippi in 42 B.C. Octavian and Mark Antony were victorious. "This defeat meant that Rome would have an imperial form of government and not a republican one. It ensured the worship of the deified dead emperor and would later be grounds for contention between the Christians and the Roman government. The Christians would refuse to worship the imperial cult."[69]

When Octavian and Antony needed a place to settle some of the veterans of the war with Cassius and Brutus, they

---

[69] Gordon Franz, "Gods, Gold, and the Glory of Philippi." at the URL: http://www.ldolphin.org/pphilippi.html.

chose Philippi and made it into a Roman Colony in honor of the victory they had won. A colony was a city established by Rome as part of its defensive strategy. Soldiers and citizens who were sent to the colonies retained their citizenship as if they were still in Rome. Thus most such cities were made up of at least two groups of people, the full citizens and the native population. Slaves made up a third group in many cities.

In 30 BC, Octavian became Roman emperor, reorganized the colony, and established more settlers there, veterans possibly from the Praetorian Guard and other Italians. The city was renamed Colonia Iulia Philippensis, and then Colonia Augusta Iulia Philippensis after January, 27 BC, when Octavian received the title Augustus from the Roman Senate. The city that Paul entered about the year 50 A.D. was a proud Roman colonial city full of families with ties to the Roman military.

The Location of the City

On the northern shore of the Mediterranean, the Aegean Sea lies between Greece and Macedonia on the west and Asia Minor on the east. Philippi is situated some ten miles inland from the Mediterranean near the northern end of the Aegean Sea.

Travelers moving from the east to the west (as were Paul, Silas and Luke) could either walk around the northern end of the Aegean Sea (and take a boat for the short crossing of the Dardanelles or the Bosporus) or cross the Aegean Sea by boat. Troas was the harbor from which the boats left to cross over to Philippi. It was the terminus of the major roads across Asia Minor and thus a busy port city. It was here that Paul and Silas apparently met Luke and where Paul had his vision of the Macedonian man calling him to help. The voyage from Troas to Philippi was a two day voyage in good weather when the winds were favorable. The boat on which Paul and his group travelled left Troas and in one day of sailing stopped for the night on the island of Samothrace.

The next day the group made the short voyage around the island of Thasos and landed on the Macedonian coast at Neapolis, the port city for Philippi. From there it was about a ten mile walk to Philippi. There was one superhighway that stretched all the way across Macedonia and it went right through Philippi and Neapolis. This was the famous Via Egnatia, the Egnatian Way. The fact that the Via Egnatia touched the Aegean coast line at Neapolis alllowed this city to become a major hub for travel between Rome and Istanbul and points further east. Travelers could decide here whether to walk around the end of the Aegean Sea or take a ship across the Sea. It was such a famous hub that one could almost expect to hear Jack Benny's announcer, Mel Blanc, announcing "Train leaving on Track Five for Anaheim, Azusa and Cuck…..amonga."

The Layout of the City

Of course we don't have any pictures of what Philippi looked like in Paul's time and much of the architectural remains that have been excavated come from the centuries after Paul as attested by the presence of Christian basilicas there. Nevertheless, Roman and Greek cities had much the same layout throughout the Mediterranean and Roman world. Some things were constants. There would always be a central forum or market place and normally there would be a theatre. There would be a grid like structure to the city with major north-south and east-west highways. There would be a colonnaded walkway on either side of the main road with shops lining the walkway. There would be a public bath. And, of course, there would be a temple or temples dedicated to the gods worshipped in the city.

The Via Egnatia cut diagonally through town forming the main street of the city. The forum in the center of the city was an open area surrounded by municipal buildings including a library. Much of the governance of the city took place in this open area. Adjacent to the forum another open space was the market area for the city called in Greek an agora. Luke says that Paul and Silas were brought into the agora to face the magistrates (Acts 16:19) after local business men complained that these Jews were "disturbing our city." The theatre in Philippi was across the street from the agora along with one or more temples. They had a gym in Philippi. On the plan of the excavation it is listed as the "palaestra." The name itself comes from the Greek word for wrestling. It was the area devoted to exercise and competition, especially wrestling. One ancient author in his book about architecture describes a palaestra as

> square or rectangular in shape with colonnades along all four sides creating porticoes. The portico on the northern side of the palaestra was of double depth to protect against the weather. Big halls (exedrae) were built along the single depth sides of the palaestra with seats for those enjoying intellectual pursuits, and the double depth side was divided into an area for youth activities (ephebeum), a punching bag area (coryceum), a room for applying powders (conisterium), a room for cold bathing, and an oil storeroom (elaeothesium). ...During the Roman Imperial period the palaestra was often combined with, or joined to, a bath.[70]

The Religious Culture of the City

When Paul, Silas and Luke walked through the city gates of ancient Philippi about the year 50 A.D. they could well have said of these people what Paul later said of the Athenians:

---

[70] Vetruvius, *On Architecture* cited from the web site at the URL: https://en.wikipedia.org/wicki/Palaestra.

"I perceive in every way you are very religious. For as I passed along, and observed the objects of your worship, I found also an altar with this inscription, 'To an unknown god.'"

Philippi was certainly not "un-churched." Some of the citizens who had come from the Thracian region (the northern part of the Macedonian region) worshiped Thracian deities, especially the Thracian Horseman. The Thracian Horseman was a god of the underworld usually depicted on funeral statues as a horseman slaying a beast with a spear. Greek settlers brought with them the veneration of Athena, Dionysus and Apollo. Athena was the goddess of wisdom, courage, inspiration, civilization, law and justice, just warfare, mathematics, strength, strategy, the arts, crafts, and skill. The people of Athens built the Parthenon to honor her! Dionysus was the god of fertility and wine. Apollo, is the god of prophecy and plagues and is sometimes associated with the Sun. The Romans brought with them Jupiter, Mars, and the emperor cult. There were ancient temples to more than one of these gods and goddesses in Philippi, but there was no Jewish synagogue in the city. Paul was in gentile territory for sure when he arrived in Macedonia.

Paul was successful in establishing a church in Philippi, but it is obvious that Christianity did not immediately supplant the many forms of worship in Philippi. The rocky Acropolis that towers over Philippi was used more than eighty times by grateful worshippers of Diana to carve her image and write of their grateful fulfillment of vows to her.[71] Thus the tiny beginnings of the church in Philippi took some three hundred years to become the dominant faith in Philippi after Constantine the Emperor accepted Christianity.[72] It is difficult to imagine the immensity of the task that faced Paul, Silas and Luke in Philippi. Massive and awesome architecture attested to the centuries of worship for the many gods of Macedonia. It took some courage for Paul to tell the Macedonians that just twenty-five years earlier, the God who created the universe had sent his Son, his very incarnation, to Israel and they crucified him. How did he ever begin to convince these people that their centuries old faiths were false?

Philippi in the Book of Acts

As is often the case, Luke's account of Paul's activity in Philippi is difficult to reconcile with Paul's letter to the Philippians. For example, Lydia is not mentioned in Paul's letter yet Luke says that Paul, Silas and Luke stayed in her home while in Philippi (Acts 16:15). Of course Paul's letter to Philippi was written several years after his first visit to the city, perhaps as many as fifteen years later. It may well be that Lydia was no longer alive or no longer in Philippi. There is no identification of the Philippian jailer who would have been Paul's first gentile

---

[71] Valerie Abrahamsen, "Christianity and the Rock Reliefs at Philippi," *Biblical Archaeologist* (March, 1988), 48

[72] Rodney Stark, *The Triumph of Christianity*, (New York: HarperOne, 2011) 157, says that there were fewer than 1500 Christians in the world by 50 A.D, a figure that grew to six million by the time Constantine joined the church.

convert in Macedonia. The three or four people mentioned by Paul (Euodia, Syntyche, Clement and Epaphroditus) do not appear in the book of Acts. Obviously these people entered the picture after the time Luke describes, but it would have been helpful had Paul or Luke given us some cross references.

Lydia

The Gangites river is almost a mile west of the city, but this is where Paul found a small collection of Jewish women on his first Sabbath day in Philippi. One would get the impression from Luke that one of the women, Lydia, a god-fearer—that is, a person who though not a Jew herself had accepted the Jewish view of God and attached herself to the Jewish community—was immediately convinced to become a Christian. While this may be the case, one should always bear in mind that the events in Acts often appear to be closer together than they were. We don't know how many times Paul met with this group at the place of prayer. At any rate, Lydia was the first person in Macedonia to become a Christian. Lydia was a "seller of purple," that is, a seller of garments dyed with the purple dye made in her home town of Thyatira in Asia. Lydia had a house and thus seems to have been of some wealth. Either she was a widow or had never married because there is no mention of a husband. When she became a Christian she invited Paul and his group to stay in her home (Luke says "she prevailed upon us."). Lydia is mentioned again at the end of Paul's first visit to Philippi. When Paul and

Silas were let out of prison," they went out of the prison, and visited Lydia…"(Acts 16:40). In Paul's letter to the Philippians he mentions that they had sent him gifts. Doubtless, some of these gifts came from Lydia. It is interesting to note the role of women in the church at Philippi. Lydia was the first, but in Paul's letter he says of two other women, Euodia and Syntyche "they have labored side by side with me in the gospel…" (Philippians 4:3). How we wish Paul had expanded his note just a bit to tell us more about how these women worked with him.

The Woman Who Said More Than She Knew

On the way to the place of prayer on one occasion Paul and his group were met by a woman who worked as a fortune teller. Perhaps she was a slave; at least she was "owned" by some men who used her ability to interpret signs to earn money. When she saw Paul and his group she followed them (perhaps trying to sell them her services?) and repeatedly screamed out "These men are servants of the Most High God, who proclaim to you the way of salvation" (Acts 16:17). Had she overheard Paul discussing Christ with the women by the riverside? However she came to her information, she had it right. That is precisely what Paul was doing, but even though she told the truth, the way she told it was unacceptable to Paul and he was "annoyed." The common assumption was that such gifts as this woman had were evidence that she had a "spirit" or perhaps an "evil spirit" within her. Paul exorcised the spirit deemed to be within her and it

103

quickly became apparent to everyone that she no longer had the gift! Since she could not be rented out, her "owners" were outraged and took Paul to court.

The "court" in this case was an open air place in the Agora known as the "bema" where a magistrate would hear cases. The case presented by the "owners" so enraged the magistrates that they "tore the garments off them (Paul and Silas) and gave orders to beat them with rods" (Acts 16:22). Roman magistrates were authorized to punish those convicted and were assisted by lictors who carried out their orders. The primary lictor who served a magistrate carried a bundle of rods (with an ax attached if the magistrate had the power to execute) as the symbol of the magistrate's power.

The Philippian Jailer

Paul and Silas were jailed after being beaten. If they tried to invoke their rights as a Roman citizen they were not heard. The room below ground level[73] that served as a prison in Philippi has been excavated and may well have been the very cell in which Paul was kept. Luke tells us that on the night they were imprisoned there was an earthquake—not an unheard of event in this part of the world. The earthquake loosened walls and allowed shackles to come free of their moorings but Paul and Silas did not flee. The jailer who was charged with keeping them was overwhelmed by their refusal to flee and immediately became

---

[73] Acts 16:34 says the jailer "brought them up into his house."

receptive to what Paul had already said to him. He and those of his household were baptized that very night—Luke does not tell us how much water they used. It would be very interesting to know whether the jailer was still in Philippi when Paul wrote his letter!

Departure from Philippi

The next morning, after the earthquake and the events surrounding the conversion of the Jailer, the magistrates sent word to release the prisoners. We aren't told why they made this decision. Paul, however, who was a Roman citizen refused to leave the prison without a public apology from the magistrate which he got. After the apology, however, the magistrates asked Paul and Silas to leave the city so their work there was cut short. They had a brief visit with Lydia and the "brethren" and then left the city. It isn't clear just how long Paul was in Philippi but the work he did in that period produced a church that was alive and well more than a decade later. And it was this group of people of whom Paul said

> I thank my God in all my remembrance of you, always in every prayer of mine for you all making my prayer with joy, thankful for your partnership in the gospel from the first day until now. And I am sure that he who began a good work in you will bring it to completion at the day of Jesus Christ....I hold you in my heart, for you are all par-

takers with me of grace, both in my imprisonment and in the defense and confirmation of the gospel. (Philippians 1: 3-7)

The Legacy of Philippi

It may well be that the greatest work the church at Philippi ever did was to draw forth from Paul the magnificent letter he wrote. It has been treasured by Christians ever since he wrote it. It has often served to inspire and encourage because it sings to our souls. Listen to just a few of the words to Lydia, Euodia, Syntyche, Clement, Epaphroditus and the rest of the brethren:

To me to live is Christ and to die is gain.

Have this mind among yourselves which is yours in Christ Jesus, who though he was in the form of God, did not count equality with God a thing to be grasped, but emptied himself....that at the name of Jesus every knee should bow, in heaven and on earth and under the earth.

Whatever gain I had, I counted as loss for the sake of Christ...For his sake I have suffered the loss of all things, and count them as refuse, in order that I may gain Christ...

Forgetting what lies behind and straining forward to what lies ahead, I press on toward the goal for the prize of the upward call of God in Christ Jesus.

Rejoice in the Lord always; again I will say Rejoice

It is the word of God for the people of God. Thanks be unto God.

Chapter 8

Thessalonica: The City That Made Paul Think

It may be stretching things just a bit to say that Thessalonica-more than other cities in which Paul ministered--made a thinker of Paul, but there is no doubt that Paul's thinking about the resurrection of the dead was shaped by this city and its Christians. Paul's two letters to the Christians of this city contain our earliest window on his mind because, as far as we know, they are his first letters to a church. They deal with practical matters, but their most memorable sections deal with serious questions raised by this early Christian congregation. Paul had no commentaries to consult, no body of doctrine to guide him, no fellow pastors who had handled these questions before him. The Christians of Thessalonica required Paul to break new ground and give them the benefit of his thinking about how death affected a Christian's relationship with God. For at least two thousand years Paul's thinking has been God's word for Christians around the world. That's why we call it inspired.

Where is Thessalonica?

Thessalonica is a hundred miles southwest of Philippi. It would have taken Paul's group about a week to make the journey to Thessalonica provided they did not stop in any of the towns along the way.[74]   Luke mentions that the group passed through Amphipolis and Apollonia which means that they walked below the two large lakes they passed. The modern road goes north of the lakes. There were several towns along the way that Luke does not mention; he singled out Amphipolis and Apollonia perhaps because they were the largest cities on the route.   Amphipolis at one point was a regional capital after Alexander the Great's empire was divided up. Amphipolis nestled beneath its Acropolis in the bend of the river Strymon. The city's name—"Amphi-polis,"   means something like "around the city" referring to the river which formed a horseshoe bend around Amphipolis. It was a major stopping point on both the old Macedonian royal highway and the Roman Egnatian Way which means it was located on the Route 66 or Interstate 20/59 of its day.   Amphipolis was about 32 miles west of Philippi and 3 miles from the Aegean Sea. It was roughly the same distance from Philippi that Apollonia was from Thessalonica so these may well have been logical stopping places between the two cities.   Apollonia was also on the Via Egnatia, the Roman highway that crossed all the way from the western coast of Macedonia to the city that we know of as Istanbul.   Today Apollonia is a small village, with no more than a couple dozen homes clustered around a few roads. We can't know what was there in Paul's day, but it is quite

---

[74] A nice web site dealing with Paul's walk from Philippi to Thessalonica may be found at: http://www.hosannakerrville.org/learning-center.html

likely that there were inns and a bath of some sort which travelers could use. Today we stop at a Cracker Barrel or a Red Lobster for lunch just off the interstate, but Paul and his group would have had little other than bread, olives, and perhaps figs or dates while on the road.

Why Thessalonica?

When Paul and his companions left Philippi they headed west on the Via Egnatia, the major Roman road across Macedonia. We have no way of knowing whether Paul intended originally to go on to Thessalonica. Perhaps this was another case of making lemonade from the lemons life handed him. But Thessalonica was the largest city in Macedonia and the capital of its region. Paul's method generally was to go to the capital cities, so it is quite possible that when he heard the call to Macedonia, he thought in terms not of Philippi but of Thessalonica.

Thessalonica was founded about 315 BC by King Cassander of Macedon, who named it after his wife Thessalonikeia, a half-sister of Alexander the Great. Little is known about her except that she was born under favorable circumstances — her father, Philip II, had just conquered Thessaly. He named his daughter "victory (niki or nica) in Thessaly." [75]

---

[75] Cited from the Hosanna Lutheran Church's website; see footnote 74.

In addition to its importance in the Greek world and in Macedonia in particular, there was another major reason why Paul pressed on toward this goal. Thessalonica had a large Jewish population and a synagogue. In fact, it seems to have had not only a Jewish synagogue but perhaps also a Samaritan synagogue. An inscription was found there which has the priestly blessing ("The Lord bless you and keep you....) written in Samaritan. Since the Jews and the Samaritans were hostile to each other, this could not have come from a Jewish synagogue—hence, the conclusion that there was once a Samaritan synagogue in Thessalonica. In the first century A.D. there were many Samaritans in various places. On the island of Delos in the Aegean Sea two inscriptions have been found which document that a Samaritan community flourished there in the first century A.D. [76] So in addition to the Christians, Jews, Samaritans, and disciples of John the Baptist are all known to have spread throughout the Roman empire.

The Jewish community in Thessalonica appears to have been a large one. Jews lived in the southwestern quarter of the city. "The Southwestern Quarter was home to most of the foreigners who'd settled in Thessalonica, African-Greeks and Jews who'd moved from Alexandria, Egypt two centuries before. ...The foreigners themselves lived nearest to the Sea Wall by the western side of the shoreline, where the anchorage

---

[76] Reinhard Pummer, *The Samaritans in Flavius Josephus* (Tübingen, Germany: Mohr Sievbeck, 2009) 17.

was deepest and most large ships docked. The strong Jewish community lived mainly in this southwest quarter as well, having built their synagogue near the sea, which was outside the original walls at the time, but now stood just within the Sea Wall built after 42 BC."[77]

The Jewish community in Thessalonica was led by a Chief Rabbi (called the Ruler of the Synagogue) and there were several other rabbis who served as teachers. There was a lay council of elders or rulers who advised the Chief Rabbi. The members of the Jewish community

"adopted the Greek language, although retaining many words of Hebrew or Aramaic origin, as well as the Hebrew script. Performing their religious rites in perfect freedom, they quickly acquired considerable influence and gladly welcomed all the Gentiles who cared to approach them, without requiring any preliminary rites of initiation. There thus grew up alongside the Jewish community a small group of converts to monotheism. This then was the organized Hebrew community in the Thessaloniki of the earliest Christian period, the community which was visited by the Apostle Paul. And it was his journey, as described in the Acts of the Apostles, which pro-

---

[77] Bill Heroman at http://www.thessalonica.net/2005/03/layout.html

vided the first documentary evidence of the existence of a Jewish community in Thessaloniki: " they came to Thessalonica, where was a synagogue of the Jews. And Paul, as his manner was, went in unto them, and three sabbath days reasoned with them out of the scriptures."[78]

Thus Thessalonica offered Paul the opportunity to speak to large numbers of people who knew the Old Testament (in Greek, as Paul did) and who already expected the coming of a Messiah. Paul spent several weeks in Thessalonica urging them to believe that Jesus was the Messiah who suffered as the Old Testament had said he would and rose from the dead. Some did but many did not as we shall see when we turn to Luke's account of the events in Thessalonica.

What Happened in Thessalonica?

How Does Luke Know?

The story of what happened is told by Luke in Acts 17. Very little in the two letters of Paul to the Thessalonians helps us fill out the picture Luke provided. When we looked at the events in Philippi earlier, we noted that Luke wrote as if he

---

[78] Albertos Nar, "Social Organization and Activity of the Jewish Community in Thessaloniki," extracted from *Queen of the Worthy, Thessaloniki, History and Culture*, Volume I, History and Culture ed. I.K. Hassiotis, Paratiritis, 1997, 266-295 and cited from http://www.macedonian- heritage.gr/Contributions/ 20010704_ Nar.html.

were personally present there. In Acts 16, Luke repeatedly says "We" in describing what happened in Troas and Philippi. Luke does not describe the events in Thessalonica in the first person leading some to wonder if he stayed behind in Philippi. Some have surmised that Luke's home was in Philippi since the next time he wrote that "We" did something is in Acts 20:6: "we sailed away from Philippi … ." If Luke was present in Thessalonica, he does not tell us so.

How Long Was Paul There?

We do not know how long Paul labored in Thessalonica. Luke mentions that "for three weeks" –literally "three Sabbaths"--Paul argued his case in the synagogue. This may mean that Paul's stay in Thessalonica was a month or less but when he wrote to the Philippians he remembered that they "sent me help once and again" (Philippians 4:16). This seems to imply that the Christians in Philippi sent money to Paul several times while he was in Thessalonica. In Paul's first letter to the Thessalonians he mentions that "we worked night an day, that we might not burden any of you" (I Thessalonians 2:9). We have no way of knowing how much Paul earned for his work, but whatever it was, it apparently needed to be supplemented several times. This may mean that Paul worked in Thessalonica over some months, but this is not certain. It should always be kept in mind that Luke tends to "telescope" things that happened over a long period so they appear to be closer together than they really are.

Where Did Paul Live in Thessalonica?

In Philippi Paul was taken in by Lydia, the seller of purple cloth. In Thessalonica, apparently Paul's host was a man named Jason. We are not told anything about Jason except that he had a house and that he had "received" Paul and his group. Whether this means that he employed Paul or just befriended him we don't know, but Luke leaves the impression that Jason was one of the Christian "brethren" in Thessalonica. At the end of the letter Paul wrote to the Romans he mentions that Jason is with him. Presumably this is the same man who, along with other Macedonians, was traveling with Paul as he took an offering to the church in Jerusalem.

What Was His Message?

Paul's message to the Jewish community in Thessalonica was the same message he delivered in Philippi. "He argued with them from the scriptures explaining and proving that it was necessary for Christ to suffer and to rise from the dead, and saying, 'This Jesus, whom I proclaim to you, is the Christ'" (Acts 17:2-3). It is hard for those of us who live twenty centuries after these events to understand the enormity of Paul's task. Jews had been looking for the Messiah (whom they understood to be a new David who would restore Israel and rule over it) for hundreds of years. Every year as they celebrated the Passover they left a chair at the table empty for Elijah who would return as the forerunner of the Messiah. None of the things they expected to happen when the Messiah appeared had happened, but Paul asserted to the congregations he addressed that the Messiah had in fact appeared and that he was Jesus of Nazareth. Moreover, he described how Jesus was executed on a cross and then rose from the dead. You can imagine the skepticism he encountered. If a person arrived at our church this week and announced that the Messiah had returned and that he was arrested, imprisoned and executed as a revolutionary, you know that we would say, "That can't be!" The return of the Messiah will introduce the final judgment and none of the things we expect to be part of the end times has occurred! So it was when Paul preached "Christ and him crucified." He went back through the Old Testament and used passages like Isaiah 52-53 which speaks of one who "was bruised for our iniquities…and with his stripes we are healed" to show that the Messiah's suffering should have been expected. It would be interesting to know all the Old Testament passages Paul used in proving that Jesus was the Messiah.

Who Were the Devout Greeks?

Luke tells us that some of the Thessalonian Jews were persuaded. He mentions also that "a great many of the devout Greeks" were persuaded. In every Jewish community all over the Roman empire there were Gentiles who accepted the Old

Testament and became part of the synagogue family. Most of these did not actually convert to Judaism, but they were accepted as part of the family. Their relationship must have been something like those who come under the "watchcare"[79] of a Baptist church but do not officially join. They are sometimes called "God-fearers." These Gentiles shared religious ideas with Jews; they accepted many of the Jewish religious ideas and practices but did not accept all the food laws and the males were not circumcised. Apparently many of Paul's converts to the Christian faith came from these God-fearers.[80]

What Kind of Women Believed?

A third group mentioned by Luke as those who accepted Paul's message—Luke says that "not a few" of these became Christians—were the "leading women." In both the Gospel of Luke and in Acts, Luke goes out of his way to emphasize the role the women played as Jesus' disciples and in the early churches. Some interpreters take these "leading women" to be the wives of the "devout Greeks," but it seems

---

[79] Or is the term "pastoral care."

[80] "One striking if not stunning example [of evidence for these gentile synagogue adherents] is a list of financial donors on the synagogue door at Aphrodisias, a city east of Ephesus in modern Turkey. It has 126 names and distinguishes three separate groups: 55 percent are Jews, 2 percent are "converts," and 43 percent are those synagogue adherents who are explicitly called "God-worshippers" (9 of them were members of the city council)." Marcus J. Borg and John Dominic Crossan, *The First Paul* (New York: Harper One, 2009), p. 87.

more likely that these women were persons of wealth and influence who, like Lydia, accepted Paul's message and contributed to his work. One such woman, Phoebe from Cenchreae, the port city of Corinth, is mentioned in Paul's letter to the Romans (16:1-2). Phoebe is called a "helper" (Greek: *prostatis*). Inscriptions found indicate "that women of wealth could and did hold influential positions in the society of Paul's lifetime, and that the title *prostatis* and cognate words designated such actions."[81] Luke does not give this title to the women in Thessalonica, but he does call them "leading" women. These are women who would belong to the "first" families of Thessalonica. Luke wants us to know that not all of the early Christians were slaves or uneducated poor people. "It is much more probable than not that at least some of these leading and prominent Christian women participated in the political and economic life of their city."[82]

How Did Paul's Stay Conclude?

Thessalonica was a "free city." This means that it was not ruled directly by Roman authorities but had its own admin-

---

[81] R. A. Kearlsey, "Women in Public Life in the Roman East: Iunia Theodora, Claudia Metrodora and Phoebe, Benefactress of Paul," (Tyndale Bulletin 50.2 (1999) 189-211). See the article at: http://tyndalehouse.com/tynbul/library/TynBull_1999_50_2_03_Kearsley_WomenPublicLife.pdf

[82] James M. Arlandson, "Lifesyles of the Rich and Christian: Women, Wealth, and Social Freedom," in Amy-Jill Levine, *A Feminist Companion to the Acts of the Apostles* (London: T & T Clark, 2004), p. 162.

istrators.[83] Its citizens did not become Roman citizens. Such free cities kept their independence only as long as Rome trusted the city's leadership. Both here in Acts 17 and again in Acts 19 Luke describes public officials who are super sensitive to disturbances which the Romans might interpret as seditious and bring about the loss of the city's freedom.

Luke attributes the opposition to Paul to jealous Jews who saw Paul converting the wealthy non-Jews who had been part of their synagogue. In 1 Thessalonians Paul himself noted that the Thessalonians "suffered the same things from your own countrymen" as the Judean churches did from their fellow Jews, suggesting that the opponents were non-Jews. Perhaps there was opposition from both groups, but it appears from the charge brought that the main opposition was from the Greek population. A mob gathered and attacked the home of Jason where Paul had been staying. Paul was not there at the time of the attack but Jason and some Christian believers were there and they were taken before the politarchs in the forum. The charge leveled against Jason was that he harbored a person who committed treason by acknowledging a king other than Caesar. Luke does not describe Jason's defense, but obviously the action taken by the politarchs indicated that they did not believe the charge. The politarchs made Jason and the Christians post bond which they would forfeit if there were any fur-

---

[83] Luke calls the city officials here "politarchs" (Acts 17:6) which is translated by the RSV as "authorities." Luke's term is the proper term for officials of a free city.

ther disturbance. Luke goes on to write that "the brethren immediately sent Paul and Silas away by night..."(Acts 17:10) to avoid a further provocation.

Sir William Ramsay, the nineteenth century scholar who did so much to clarify Paul's travels, noted that Paul later wrote to the Thessalonians that "we wanted to come to you—I, Paul, again and again—but Satan hindered us" (I Thessalonians 2:18). Ramsay suggested that "So long as the magistrates [politarchs] maintained this attitude, he [Paul]could not return; he was helpless, and Satan had power."[84]

Conclusion

Once again Paul was sent off on short notice in the middle of the night. At least this time he walked out and didn't have to be hidden in a basket lowered over the city wall. But since he went to Beroea it is clear that he couldn't take the main road out of town. All in all, it really wasn't a very promising start for the Church. Paul was driven out of Antioch in Pisidia by a mob; he was stoned and left for dead at Iconium; he was forbidden to preach in two provinces; and he was jailed in Philippi. In some ways the worst was yet to come. Lesser men with normal egos might have withered and withdrawn. But this was the man who reminded others, "If God be for us who can be against us!" (Romans 8:31). He had seen it all: tribulation, distress, persecution, famine, nakedness, peril

---

[84] William M. Ramsay, *St. Paul the Traveller and the Roman Citizen* (Grand Rapids: Baker Book House, 1960 [reprint of 1897 edition]) 231.

and sword and "in all these things we are more than conquerors through him who loved us!" You would have thought that every city he visited had given him a ticker tape parade and the keys of the city.

Chapter 9

Athens: The City That Laughed At Paul

Tertullian, one of the most prolific of the early theologians of the church, once exclaimed: "What has Athens to do with Jerusalem or the academy with the church?"[85] Obviously he believed philosophy to be so destructive of faith that there could be no link between Athens and Jerusalem. If only he could have known! The centuries to come after his time witnessed a virtual baptism of Greek philosophy by the Church. Augustine in the 5th century A.D. introduced the church to Plato and the idealism Plato taught is still a central part of many Christians' view of the world although they may not realize from whence their ideas have come. Then, eight hundred years after Augustine, Thomas Aquinas infused the ideas of Plato's student, Aristotle, into Catholic theology. Plato's idealism stressed that the "other world," the world that stands behind our constantly changing and imperfect world, was the real world. Aristotle insisted that we have to deal with the world we have and use our reason to help us understand God's revelation. It was largely this adoption of Aristotle that allowed

---

[85] Tertullian, *De praescriptione haereticorum* ((On the prescription of heretics), VII. See English excerpts at https://history.hanover.edu/courses/excerpts/344tert.html

science to develop in our western world to the degree it has. Thus Greek philosophy has influenced both our Christian thinking and our western world in profound ways of which most of us are completely unaware. And as far as we know, it was Paul who introduced the Christian faith to the philosophical schools of Athens. Of all the first generation Christians we know, Paul was the only one who could have studied philosophy in a Greek university city (Tarsus), the only one reared outside the constricting borders of the land of Israel and, thus, broadened by wide contact with Gentiles, and the only one equipped linguistically to engage philosophers with the Gospel in their own language, Greek. In so many ways, as Mark reminded us, it was the "fullness of time." Many of the Jews to whom Paul preached rejected both him and his message violently; in Athens they laughed. And it was here that Paul tells us that he resolved to know only "Christ, and him crucified."

The Way To Athens

Just how did Paul get to Athens? When he was quickly sent out of Thessalonica by Jason and the other Christians to avoid another mob scene, he made a decision that had far reaching consequences. Had he left Thessalonica on the interstate highway by which he entered that city, the Egnatian Way, Paul would have headed West toward Rome. This route would have taken him all the way across Macedonia to the Adriatic Sea. In Romans, Paul says that he had preached the Gospel "from Jerusalem and as far round as Illyricum" (15:19). Illyricum is the province at the western end of the Egnatian Way where Paul would have ended up had he continued on that famous highway. This time he did not choose that route though he says he did at another time about which we have no knowledge. The night he left Thessalonica the Engatian Way may not have been safe for him to walk. His friends took him out another way toward the city of Beroea (modern Veria) some forty miles away. There was a Jewish synagogue there according to the book of Acts and this may have been the determining factor in Paul's decision. Apparently the natives of Beroea responded positively to their new visitor at least until some people from Thessalonica arrived and told them of the disturbances there. We don't know how long Paul was able to teach in Beroea but it was most likely a short stay. Once again Paul was taken out of town "immediately," but he left behind two of his younger colleagues, Silas and Timothy, so apparently they were not in danger there.

Luke tells us that the Beroeans "sent Paul off on his way to the sea" but he also says that "Those who conducted Paul brought him as far as Athens..." (Acts 17:15) so it appears that a few new converts from Beroea travelled with Paul all the way to Athens. To catch a ship to Athens, Paul would have had to walk back toward Thessalonica for about twenty miles. Luke does not mention the port city from which they departed. Had Paul elected to return to the Egnatian Way a twenty mile walk would have put him on the main highway, but he obviously made a decision to go a different direction. We can't know what factors went into that decision but the attraction of the main cities of Greece, Athens and Corinth, may well have been what drew him south. It would be nice to know how long they had to wait on a boat headed for Athens and what the fare was for passengers on a freighter and whether they had to sleep on the beach while they waited and what the weather was like, but none of these details have come down to us. All we know is that the small group found a ship that took them to the port city that served Athens, Piraeus.

From Piraeus To the Gates of Athens

It was a five mile walk to Athens from the dock in Piraeus.[86] The road to Athens was flanked by a massive wall on either side since this road was the crucial link between Athens and its naval facilities. Of course massive as the fortifications were, they were not enough to keep out the Romans, so the city toward which Paul walked was now the capital of a Roman province. As the group neared Athens cemeteries lined the approaches to the city, a tribute to the heroic Greek warriors of legendary fame. Several roads converged at the gates to

---

[86] About a hundred years after Paul's visit a traveler named Pausanias wrote a detailed description of his visit to Athens. The city would not have changed dramatically in the intervening years. See his description of the approach from Piraeus at   http://www.fordham.edu/halsall/ancient/pausanias-bk1.asp. His ten volumes are title *Description of Greece*.

Athens making this a very busy spot. The Dipylon or Double Gate was a famous landmark. A gate on either side of a large rectangular building from which a major processional began each year led the traveler into the area of cemeteries known as the Keramaikos (from which we get our word "ceramics") because it had long been a work place for potters who got clay from the area.[87] Pausanias describes his surprise at the colors used in the statuary and the buildings.[88] We who are accustomed to seeing only the grey-white marble of the statues would have been delighted with the bright colors used on all the buildings.

From the Gates of Athens to the Agora

Once inside the city, the traveler "found himself on a long avenue flanked with large buildings leading eastward to the Agora (market place). The agora was the political, commercial, and social center of the ancient town, and has its equivalent in the *plateia* of the modern Mediterranean town. It consists

---

[87] Pausanius described it thus: "On entering the city there is a building for the preparation of the processions, which are held in some cases every year, in others at longer intervals. Hard by is a temple of Demeter, with images of the goddess herself and of her daughter, and of Iacchus holding a torch. On the wall, in Attic characters, is written that they are works of Praxiteles."

[88] "Above the Cerameicus and the portico called the King's Portico is a temple of Hephaestus. I was not surprised that by it stands a statue of Athena, because I knew the story about Erichthonius. But when I saw that the statue of Athena had blue eyes I found out that the legend about them is Libyan. For the Libyans have a saying that the Goddess is the daughter of Poseidon and Lake Tritonis, and for this reason has blue eyes like Poseidon." 1.14.6.

of a large open space (usually rectangular in shape) bordered by public buildings of religious and civic purpose. ...The Agora which Pausanias describes and where Paul "disputed daily with them that met him" was situated on relatively low ground just to the northwest of the Acropolis and almost directly north of the Areopagus."[89]

Today the visitor to Athens can experience something of what the Agora was like in Paul's time. The eastern end of the Agora has been restored and the long colonnaded walkway of the Stoa of Attalos offers welcome relief from the hot Greek sun. It was in one of the Stoas around the Agora that Paul would have begun his conversations with the philosophers. Luke says that he argued "in the market place (the Agora) every day with those who chanced to be there" (Acts17:17). Paul also taught and debated in the synagogue with the Jewish community but the location of the Jewish synagogue is unknown. Apparently it was outside the Agora because Luke says that Paul preached "in the agora and in the synagogue." Paul would have spent his time in the synagogue interpreting the passages in the Old Testament that pointed to role of the Messiah as a suffering servant. Today we can probably tell which scriptures Paul would have used by

---

[89] William A. McDonald, "Archaeology and St. Paul's Journeys in Greek Lands: Part II. Athens," *The Biblical Archaeologist* (Vol. IV February 1941, No. 1), *pp. 2-3*.

noting the passages quoted by Matthew, Mark and Luke as being fulfilled by Jesus. [90]

The Acropolis and Mars Hill

Paul was not a stranger to the beauty and grandeur of Greek architecture but even so he must have been overwhelmed by his first sight of the Athenian acropolis with its Parthenon and the other temples. The acropolis dominates Athens and would have been just a short walk on from the Agora in the center of the city. By the time Paul got to Athens these buildings

---

[90] "The form and content of the proclamation, the kerygma, can be recovered from the New Testament with reasonable accuracy. It recounted in brief the life, and work of Jesus Christ, His conflicts, sufferings, and death, and His resurrection from the dead; and it went on to declare that in these events the divinely guided history of Israel through long centuries had reached its climax. God Himself , had acted decisively in this way to inaugurate His kingdom upon earth. This was the core of all early Christian preaching, however it might be elaborated, illustrated, and explained. The preacher's aim was to convince his hearers that they were indeed confronted by the eternal God in His kingdom, power, and glory; that they, like all men, stood under His judgment upon what they had done and upon what they were, and that this judgment was now immediate and inescapable; further, that those who would put themselves under God's judgment would, through His mercy, find an opportunity open to them to enter upon a new life; that actually, as a result of these facts which they proclaimed, a new era in the relations between God and man had begun. Those who responded to this appeal and placed themselves under the judgment and mercy of God as declared in Jesus Christ, became members of the community, the Church, within which the new life could be lived. These members were then instructed in the ethical principles and obligations of the Christian life. This course of instruction in morals, as distinct from the proclamation of the gospel, is covered by the term "'teaching," which in Greek is didaché." C. H. Dodd, *Preaching and Teaching in the Early Church* found at http://www.religion-online.org/showarticle.asp?title=3368

were over 400 years old and no longer retained all their color and magnificence. They still represented the greatest achievement in human art and architecture known to man.

In the Agora Paul met some Greek Epicurean and Stoic philosophers and presented his case to them that Christ had been raised from the dead. The philosophers brushed him aside as a "babbler" (the RSV translation). The word is one of derision suggesting that Paul had picked up some scraps from the leavings of humanity much as a sparrow would scour the ground for crumbs.

When Paul spoke of resurrection, the Greek philosophers assumed he was talking about Jesus and another god, Anastasis, whose name meant resurrection. Thus they concluded that he was "a preacher of foreign divinities." It has become commonplace among Christians to make light of Epicureanism as the "eat, drink and be merry" philosophy but by doing so we do not do them justice. Epicurus (341-270 B.C.) wrote that "The gods are not to be feared; death cannot be felt; the good can be won; all that we dread can be conquered." "Virtue for Epicurus was a means to an end. That end is happiness. It is good to feel pleasure and to avoid pain, but one needs to apply reason to life. Sometimes pain is necessary in order to gain happiness. Other times, pleasure leads to more suffering than it is worth."[91] Stoicism can be traced back to Zeno of Citium

---

[91] Quoted from http://webspace.ship.edu/cgboer/latergreeks.html

(333-262). The name comes from the place where Zeno taught, the "Painted Stoa" in the Agora at Athens. Paul would have had much more in common with the Stoics than with the Epicureans. Stoics valued "apatheia," "the absence of passion, something not too different from the Buddhist idea of non-attachment. By passion Zeno meant uncontrolled emotion or physical desire. Only by taking this attitude, he felt, could we develop wisdom and the ability to apply it."[92] Some of the philosophers who heard Paul in the Stoa were willing to hear him further. These would have most likely been the Stoics. They invited Paul to speak to them and this gives Luke the opportunity to share with us the gist of Paul's sermon on Mars Hill.[93] Mars Hill was a rocky outcrop just below the Acropolis which went by the name Areopagus. Both the rocky outcrop and a citizens group that met there were known as the Areopagus so it is not certain that Paul actually stood on the rock to talk. He may have met with the Areopagus in some meeting hall in Athens but Christians have traditionally understood that Paul preached standing on the rock that is still visible in Athens today.

Earlier we noted that we could probably tell which Old Testament scriptures Paul would have used in debating with the Jews by looking at the passages that Luke included in Paul's sermons in the book of Acts. The sermon on Mars Hill is re-

---

[92] Quoted from http://webspace.ship.edu/cgboer/latergreeks.html

[93] The Greek god Ares for whom the hill is named in Greek was known to the Romans as Mars, thus the two names.

markable because it uses none of these passages. The very name of Jesus is missing from the sermon! Paul refers to Jesus only as "a man whom (God) has appointed" to judge the world (Acts 17:31). Paul begins his sermon by noting that in his tour around the city he has seen many statues dedicated to gods, even one to an "Unknown God." He takes that one as his starting point and says he will proclaim this God they do not know to them. He immediately asserts one of the things that many of his listeners could not accept—that this God he proclaimed was actually the creator of the world who made it according to his purposes. He went on to assert that God holds human beings accountable for their behavior. The means of this judgment is the "man whom he has appointed" and confirmed by raising him from the dead. The preaching of a "resurrection" caused many to quit listening to Paul. Luke names only two people who accepted Paul's message: Dionysius the Areopagite[94] and a woman named "Damaris." Luke does say that "others with them" accepted Paul's message. Since Paul never seems to have gone back to Athens and sent no letter to a church there, it seems safe to conclude that Paul did not found a congregation there that lasted.

---

[94] During the medieval period Saint Dionysius the Areopagite and Saint Denis of Paris were considered to be the same "Dionysius" who had been converted by Saint Paul in Acts 17:34.[10] Medieval tradition held that Saint Dionysius the Areopagite had traveled to Rome and then was commissioned by the Pope to preach in Gaul (France), where he was martyred. Unfortunately, we know nothing about the man Paul converted.

After Athens

Paul left Athens and went on to Corinth where his ministry was much more successful. In a letter to the Corinthians written later, Paul reflected on his experience in Athens. Here is what he wrote:

"When I came to you, brethren, I did not come proclaiming to you the testimony of God in lofty words of wisdom. For I decided to know nothing among you except Jesus Christ and him crucified....my speech and my message were not in plausible words of wisdom, but in demonstration of the Spirit and of power, that your faith might not rest in the wisdom of men but in the power of God." (I Corinthians 2:1-5)

Paul sounds like a man who failed. He tried to speak to Greeks on their own terms, and he did not make much headway. Surely there are few preachers who have not had an experience like that of Paul. The sense of failure in such a crucial situation stays with a person long after his reason tells him that he did all he could have done. Indeed we may still hear echoes of Paul's experience in Athens in a letter which seems to have been written near the end of his life from prison in Rome in which he asks Christians to pray for him

"that utterance may be given me in opening my

mouth boldly to proclaim the mystery of the gospel, for which I am an ambassador in chains; that I may declare it boldly, as I ought to speak." (Ephesians 6:19-20)

It may well be that Paul's hard time in Athens ultimately produced great fruit, however, since Paul's message of the crucified Christ obviously found a place in many Greek hearts in the years after Athens. So what should we say in response to Tertullian? What does Athens have to do with Jerusalem? It has everything to do with Jerusalem just as do Antioch and Iconium, Philippi and Corinth. "There is neither Jew nor Greek, there is neither slave nor free, there is neither male nor female; for you are all one in Christ Jesus" (Galatians 3:28) One heart beats in them all and one message reaches out to all. [95]

---

[95] For a beautiful photographic tour of Athens and other sites in Greece, "Smithsonian Magazine Presents Rick Steves Tour of Greece " may be found at: http://microsite.smithsonianmag.com/content/Rick-Steves/video/ #ooid=ltY2VhMTq2sywD-7Ry8HF7BFaLJ2T0Ah.

Chapter 10

Corinth: The City Paul Taught How To Love

In the minds of ordinary Christians, Corinth may well be the city they most associate with the Apostle Paul. Although Romans is longer and comes before the Corinthian letters in our New Testament, many Christians find Romans hard to read and move on quickly to the Corinthian correspondence. There are enough thorny ethical issues involved in Corinth to make a modern soap opera seem tame by comparison. The first letter opens with the fact that the church is deeply divided by allegiances to former pastors, especially Peter, Paul and Apollos and with that level of pastoral excellence it might be hard for people not to have a favorite. Paul has been informed that a man in the congregation is living with his father's wife and Paul demands that this person be removed from the congregation (1 Cor. 5:3-5). Some members of the church were so upset by the business dealings with other church members that they had taken them to court, a move that saddened Paul (1 Cor. 6:1-8). Apparently some church members continued to visit prostitutes, perhaps those associated with one of the temples for which Corinth was famous (1 Cor. 6:12-20). The church actually wrote Paul and asked this unmarried apostle his position on sexual relationships between husbands and wives as well as those between unmarried persons (1 Cor. 7). The list goes on and on. One major issue that may seem somewhat trivial to us but which surely was not so to the Corinthian Christians was the decision each had to make about buying meat from the meat market in town, meat that had previously been dedicated to one of the pagan gods in one of the temples (1 Cor. 8-10). The issue of women's equality with men was as important in Corinth as it still is today (1 Cor. 11). And, of course, the way the Lord's Supper was observed became a problem for the First Church of Corinth (1 Cor. 11:17-34).

But even with all the attention these issues generate, few would argue that they are the high point of the letter we call 1 Corinthians. That honor clearly goes to Paul's unforgettable treatment of the gifts of the spirit and, within those three chapters (12-14), his beautiful and inspired chapter on love (1 Cor. 13). Yes, "faith, hope, love abide, these three; but the greatest of these is love." So for me, Corinth will remain the city that Paul taught about love. Thanks be to God for Corinth.

We have the good fortune to have access to ancient Corinth, and it has been fully excavated[96] so we'll take some time to locate Corinth both geographically and chronologically

---

[96] The American School of Classical Studies at Athens began the excavation of ancient Corinth in 1896. The city had been completely destroyed by an earthquake in 1858; New Corinth was built a couple of miles away leaving this site available for archaeological excavation.

135

in Paul's ministry. Then we will explore this city where Paul labored so effectively. Some of the places mentioned in Paul's letter can actually be identified with fair certainty, and this is a rare thing.

Just Where Was Corinth?

When Paul arrived in Corinth about the year 50 A.D., it was a major city in Greece. It owed its size and dominance to its location. A quick look at a large map of the Mediterranean shows that Corinth is located on the north side of a very narrow isthmus that connects mainland Greece to the area known as the Peloponnese. The distance from Athens to Corinth was about fifty miles and would have taken Paul four or five days to walk, but if one wished to take a ship from Athens to Corinth it meant sailing all the way around the Peloponnese in waters that could be treacherous. To avoid that long voyage, the Roman emperor Nero started digging a canal across the narrow isthmus that separated the Aegean from the Ionian Sea but the project was abandoned. The canal was not actually dug until modern times, but centuries before Nero, the Greeks had devised a substitute method of rolling ships across the isthmus on a track.[97] It was slow work and this meant that sailors had

---

[97] The track used for transporting ships was known as the Diolkos (from two words "across" and "portage") and was built perhaps as early as the 8th century B.C. (the time of Isaiah, Hosea and Amos in Israel). The track was almost five miles long. It is not known exactly how the ships were carried but ruts in the stone suggest that the ships were rolled on a dolly of some sort pulled by men or animals.

some time on their hands in Corinth while their ships were being towed across the land barrier. It does not take much imagination to conjure up the nightly scene in Corinth that involved drunken orgies and wild parties. It was to this bustling city with its monopoly on trade that Paul made his way while waiting for his companions Silas and Timothy to catch up to him. Doubtless Paul reasoned that what was preached in Corinth would be quickly spread across the Greek and Roman world because of the heavy flow of trade and traffic through the city. Perhaps also Paul reasoned that he could make more converts in the working world of Corinth than in the philosophical schools of Athens.

When Did Paul Get There?

Dating the missionary journeys of Paul has been problematic, but because he went to Corinth and because he appeared before the Proconsul Gallio there (Acts 18:12-17), scholars have determined that Paul was in Corinth in 50-51 A.D. Luke tells us that Paul stayed in Corinth eighteen months (Acts 18:11). We know he arrived in Corinth near the end of or after 49 A.D. because he met some people in Corinth who had been expelled from Rome by the Emperor Claudius in that year (Acts 18:2) and they had had time to move to Corinth and set up a business. Archaeologists working at the Temple of Apollo in Delphi in the 19th century found nine fragments of an inscription written by the Emperor Claudius in which he mentions the Proconsul Gallio. The inscription is dated in Claudius' 12th year. He became emperor on January 25, 41 so his twelfth year would have extended from January 25, 52 to January 24, 53. Gallio's one year term would have run from July 51 to June 52. Thus it is likely that Paul stood before the Proconsul Gallio during the summer months of 51 A.D. Luke says he stayed on for some time after that hearing. Since he left by boat and the sailing season ended with November, Paul probably left Corinth by the fall of A.D. 51.[98]

What Did Paul See When He Got To Corinth?

The Temple of Aphrodite

As Paul approached Corinth coming from Athens in the east he would have walked by a truly imposing sight. Towering high above ancient Corinth stood its acropolis. Athens was not the only Greek city to have an acropolis and the Corinth Acropolis was one of the most impressive in all of Greece. The walls of Corinth always surrounded the city but in earlier times they climbed the steep acropolis to include its lofty peak within the protected zone. Like Athens, Corinth's acropolis had its temple too, a temple dedicated to Aphrodite, goddess of love. It was this association of sex and city that gave Corinth its bawdy reputation over the centuries. Here is the way William Barclay described it:

---

[98]http://reformedperspectives.org/files/reformedperspectives/new_testamen t/NT.Gordan.DatingofPaulatCorinth.6.8.04.pdf. Gardner Gordon, "Paul, Dating and Corinth: The Gallio Inscription and Pauline Chronology."

Above the isthmus towered the hill of the Acropolis, and on it stood the great temple of Aphrodite, the goddess of love. To that temple there were attached one thousand priestesses who were sacred prostitutes, and in the evenings they descended from the Acropolis and plied their trade upon the streets of Corinth, until it became a Greek proverb, 'It is not every man who can afford a journey to Corinth.' In addition to these cruder sins, there flourished far more recondite vices, which had come in with the traders and the sailors from the ends of the earth, until Corinth became not only a synonym for wealth and luxury, drunkenness and debauchery, but also for filth."[99]

The City Gates

Since Corinth was located on the narrow isthmus of land that separated the Saronic Gulf on the south and the Corinthian Gulf on the north, it was served by two port cities. On the south the port city was Cenchreae. On the Corinthian Gulf side the port city was Lechaion. As Paul made his way from Athens to Corinth on foot, he probably followed the same route that the tourist, Pausanias, used a few years later. Pausanias described the route as flanked by several tombs. He mentions the tomb of Di-

---

[99] William Barclay, *The Letters To The Corinthians*, 2-3. (The number of priestesses may be more accurate for the early days of the temple, but there were apparently enough to go around. Recent scholars have argued that by Paul's time the temple was a much smaller operation.)

ogenes of Sinope and Lais. The latter tomb is that of a famous prostitute from Corinth. There were two gates entering the city from the south and east, the Cenchreae Gate and the Southeast Gate. We don't know which Paul would have used so we will assume that he used the Cenchreae Gate.

The Agora and the Central City

The city Paul walked into had a long history. It had been conquered by the Romans about 175 B.C. and re-founded as a new city in 44 B.C., about a hundred years before Paul got there. The city was laid out on a rectangular grid covering about a half mile by a mile and a half. The city was 58 blocks from west to east and thirteen blocks from north to south. One main road fifty feet wide, the Cardo Maximus, ran north and south through the center of the city. The center of the city as in all Greek and Roman cities was an open area known as the Agora. Since Paul entered the city from the south and east he would have passed through the South Stoa, a building with many offices and a long colonnaded porch that faced into the open square of the Agora. It would have looked like the Stoa of Attalus in Athens which Paul had just visited. Once inside the Agora he saw a large open area with many altars and statues. Pausanias, describes each of the pieces that Paul would have seen and tells the story behind each of them. Across the Agora on the north side, Paul could see the main entrance to the Agora called the Propylaea. When Pausanias saw it a century after Paul the Propylaea had two golden chariots on top of its arches. These probably weren't there in Paul's time, but the great arch spanning the road north to Lechaion was there. A stone with the word "synagogue" was found near the Propylaea when the archaeologist cleared this area. It may be later than the time of Paul but doubtless indicates that the earlier synagogue in which Paul taught was in that same area.[100]

The Judgment Seat (Bema)

Midway across the Agora from the South Stoa there was a row of shops with an open platform area in the middle of the shops. From these shops there were stairs descending to the lower level of the north part of the Agora. The platform was called the "bema" and on it would have sat magistrates as they heard cases brought to them. The litigants would have stood on the lower level. Before Paul left Corinth he came to know the bema quite well as we shall see.

---

[100] At the foot of these steps an especially interesting inscription turned up — a long heavy block, apparently the upper lintel of a doorway (Fig. 11). On it there are still visible seven Greek letters which may be confidently restored and translated "Synagogue of the Jews." The careless style of the lettering, indicates that the inscription, and presumably the synagogue to which it belonged, is considerably later than the time of St. Paul. But it is reasonable to conclude that both this and the earlier one, in which the Apostle "reasoned .... every Sabbath and persuaded the Jews and the Greeks" {Acts 18:4), were located in this area. No existing foundation has yet been convincingly associated with the lintel." William A. Mcdonald, "Archaeology And St. Paul's Journeys In Greek Lands, Part III — Corinth" *Biblical Archaeologist* (Volume 5, 1942, Number 3), 41.

The Meat Market

Somewhere along the road to Lechaion and after one passed through the Propylaea Corinthians bought their groceries, especially their meats. Archaeologists discovered an inscription placed on the market there by its builder, one Quintus Cornelius Secundus, but the inscription had been broken into several pieces that were discovered in different locations. Thus the exact location of the market area can't be determined, but it was likely located in the row of shops on the Lechaion road. The inscription mentions both a meat market *(macellum* in Latin) and a fish market. This find holds special interest for us because Paul refers to a "macellum" in 1 Corinthians 10:25: "Eat whatever is sold in the meat market *(macellō* in Greek)without raising any question on the ground of conscience. " As you may remember, some Christians felt that eating meat reflected badly on them because most of the meat available had been sacrificed in one of the pagan temples in Corinth. The excess meat that could not be consumed by the priests and the worshippers in the temples was sold in the meat markets. Eating any meat then would have involved at least a second hand identification with one of the pagan gods. Paul assured them that such meat was not tainted—but he also pointed out that he would not eat it if he thought it would cause a fellow Christian problems.

The Fountain of Peirene

One of the most famous features of Corinth was its central fountain, Peirene. The Roman tourist, Pausanias, wrote that " A little farther away from the gateway[Propylaea], on the right as you go in, is a bronze Heracles. After this is the entrance to the water of Peirene. The legend about Peirene is that she was a woman who became a spring because of her tears shed in lamentation for her son Cenchrias, who was unintentionally killed by Artemis. The spring is ornamented with white marble, and there have been made chambers like caves, out of which the water flows into an open-air well. It is pleasant to drink…" The spring may have been spruced up after Paul's time but it remained the one place that everyone associated with Corinth. Neither Paul nor Luke tell us that the spring played any part in Paul's stay in Corinth but he would have known it well, passed it often and drunk many times from its cool waters.

Paul's Ministry in Corinth

We've alluded already to many of the things that transpired in Corinth which Paul himself mentions in some way in his letters. In addition to the complex situations addressed by Paul in his correspondence with Corinth (obviously written when he was somewhere else, perhaps in Ephesus on the third journey), Luke gives us some tantalizing tidbits about other events in Corinth during Paul's stay.

The Ruler of the Synagogue

Luke says that after more than a year long ministry, the Jews turned against Paul and pressed charges against him. Paul was taken to the Agora and placed before the Bema where Gallio, Rome's Proconsul, sat. What transpired there is less than crystal clear. Luke tells us that a "Ruler" of the synagogue named Crispus had accepted Paul's presentation about Jesus being the Christ. The word "Ruler" implies that Crispus was a major benefactor of the synagogue, not that he was the head of the Jewish community. In fact, Crispus was most likely not a Jew but a wealthy Gentile who had been attracted by Judaism but had not converted completely. Luke tells us that when the Jews rejected Paul's message, Paul quit going to the synagogue. He moved into the home of Titius Justus who was a Gentile and lived next door to the synagogue. It is in this context that Luke says that Crispus became a Christian. Doubtless when a major contributor to the synagogue became a Chistian, this deprived the synagogue of sorely needed funds. It may well have caused the Jewish community to press charges against Paul. When the charge was presented to Gallio, however, the Proconsul summarily dismissed the charge as an internal Jewish matter to be handled by the Jewish community. He in essence gave the Jewish community permission to punish Paul and his group which they did; they began to beat them. We would have expected Luke to say that they beat Paul and, perhaps, Crispus, but Luke instead says that the Jews beat Sosthenes whom he also calls a "Ruler of the Synagogue." Is it possible that there were two prominent Gentile contributors who had sided with Paul or is this Sosthenes the same person as Crispus? Either way, it is easy to understand why Jewish feelings were running very high against Paul.

144

At least one and perhaps two of their major non-Jewish benefactors had become Christians and were now helping the church get established.

A House Church

Christians today routinely meet in churches built especially for their worship, but the new Christians Paul brought together to form churches all across the Roman world did not have buildings for their new faith. Christianity was not a "sanctioned" religion in the Roman world. (That's why it was helpful for Christians to be recognized as part of the Jewish community in the early days. The Jewish religion was a legally protected one in the eyes of the Romans.) Christians met in homes. We normally think of the early Christians as poor, perhaps slaves, but we know that Paul's preaching led at least two and perhaps three prominent Gentiles who owned homes in Corinth to become Christians. It would have been in homes like those belonging to Titius Justus, Crispus and Sosthenes that the earliest churches met. They were the only ones big enough to hold more than a few who gathered for worship. Archaeologists have studied the remains of several homes from the first century to see if they could determine how many people were involved in Paul's churches. As it turns out one large, obviously wealthy, home was discovered in Corinth. This home had the traditional open air atrium as well as a dining area with benches where guests could recline, called a triclinium. Even in the wealthy homes these areas were in the range of sixteen by twenty feet. Scholars estimate that at most they could have accommodated forty to fifty people. It is clear from the people Paul names in his letters that some wealthy people became Christians and, obviously, they allowed their homes to be used for Christian gatherings. The fact that Roman hosts routinely had to put favored guests in the dining room and allocate other guests to the atrium may help us understand the problems the Corinthians had in eating the Lord's Supper. The fact that the church probably had to meet in several homes as Christians grew in numbers may have been a factor in the various "factions" which Paul heard existed at Corinth.

Aquila and Priscilla

Last but not least, let's talk about Aquila and Priscilla. At least the husband and perhaps both husband and wife were tentmakers as was Paul. They had been in Rome but the Roman Emperor Claudius expelled the Jews from the city. It may well have been that dissention in the Jewish community over Jesus the Messiah caused the Emperor to expel the whole community; we don't know for sure. If so this would mean that Christianity arrived in Rome at least some time before the year 49 when the Jews were expelled. Aquila and Priscilla had moved from Rome to Corinth and had a shop in down town Corinth—in the Agora-- where Paul found them. They were to spend years working together both as tentmakers and as "fishers of men." Obviously Aquila and Priscilla had already accepted Christ and were part of the Christian group in Rome. When Paul linked up with them in Corinth, the Gospel took a giant leap forward. This couple would later go with Paul to Ephesus and proved instrumental in the education of a Christian named Apollo who then became a pastor in Corinth.

Conclusion

What a story the stones of Corinth tell. We can be fairly sure that Paul walked the very streets that can still be seen there. We can be sure that the meat market and the pagan temples that furnished their meat caused Paul to think seriously about his Christian influence. We can sense the scene in the triclinium and atrium of a wealthy home in Corinth where Christians came to celebrate the Lord's Supper. But towering over the book is that thirteenth chapter about love, a chapter that tells us what human love is, not what it was reduced to in Corinth. Love was what Corinth was not but needed to become:

> [4] Love is patient and kind; love is not jealous or boastful;
> [5] it is not arrogant or rude. Love does not insist on its own way; it is not irritable or resentful;
> [6] it does not rejoice at wrong, but rejoices in the right.
> [7] Love bears all things, believes all things, hopes all things, endures all things.

Are you listening, Corinth.

Chapter 11

Ephesus: The City Where Paul Despaired

Paul tried to go to Ephesus on his second missionary journey, but when he got to the major decision point that would decide his route, he was somehow prohibited from preaching in Asia where Ephesus was located. So in the early 50's Paul spent most of his time in Corinth (at least a year and a half) after preaching in Philippi, Thessalonica, Beroea and Athens. We do not know why his obvious choice for places to preach the Gospel was denied him, but he says it was. Except for a very brief stop-over in Ephesus on the way home on his second missionary trip,[101] Paul's only time there was on his third trip.

Paul arrived in Ephesus by passing "through the upper country"—the high plateau of today's Turkey—on foot.[102] This

---

[101] In Acts 18:18-21 Luke says that Paul, Aquila and his wife Priscilla left the southern port of Corinth, Cenchreae, and headed to Syria. But then Luke notes "they came to Ephesus." and Paul left Aquila and Priscilla there. There must have been several other stops before the boat reached Ephesus and Luke tells us only that Paul spoke in the synagogue there before taking his leave. Some scholars have questioned whether this visit actually took place. At the very least, Luke's account leaves a lot of questions unanswered. No mention is made of Aquila and Priscilla in Paul's stay in Ephesus on the Third Journey.

[102] David W. J. Gill and Conrad Gempf, *The Book of Acts in Its Graeco-Roman Setting*, The Book Of Acts In Its First Century Setting (Vol 2) (Grand Rapids: Eerdmans, 1994) 308. " two great highways led from Ephesus to the east. Firstly,

was the second time he had walked all the way across Turkey and before that he had walked a circular route through eastern and central Turkey that was almost as long. He walked into one of the most beautiful and significant cities of the ancient world sometime about 53 A.D. Ephesus had at one time been the capital of Asia, but in the first century A.D. it no longer held that honor. It was still the largest city in Asia and the capital of its region, however, and even its broken remains testify to its grandeur.

Like Corinth, Ephesus has been excavated for many years, and work continues there still. At this point only some 10-15% of the city has been excavated so there is much to keep the archaeologists busy for years to come.[103] Ephesus is easily accessible by tourists and many Americans have walked its ancient streets as did Paul. Thanks to the archaeologists there is much to see in Ephesus today, some of it dating to the very time Paul was there. We'll try to get a general feel for the whole city and then focus on the Temple of Artemis and the relationship of that religious cult to the silversmiths of Ephesus. Finally we'll think about what Luke didn't tell us about Paul's stay in Ephesus and

---

the *koine hodos*, the common highway, was a very important overland route which went from Ephesus up the Maeander Valley to Tralles, Nysa, Antiocheia and onwards to the river Euphrates and beyond.[72] Secondly, from Ephesus one could travel to Sardis and then on the ancient Persian Royal Road which went to Susa; this became the primary means of linking Ephesus with the province of Galatia."

[103] The University of Vienna began the systematic excavation of the site. In 1898, the Austrian Institute of Archeology was founded with the vision of carrying out the archaeological work at Ephesus.

also about his encounter with the entrenched self-interest of the city.

The City of Ephesus

Today the city of Ephesus lies several kilometers from the ocean, but in the first century it was much closer to the sea and had a working harbor. The river that empties into the sea at Ephesus brought enough silt from the mountains above to gradually fill in the land and leave Ephesus far from the water. This process actually happened more than once. One Roman emperor moved the whole city to higher ground and then had to force the citizens to leave their homes and occupy the new city. In Paul's time, however, Ephesus was blessed by a favorable location where major roads converged and where ships from Egypt and Greece stopped. " As well as having good land routes to the north and the south, two great highways led from Ephesus to the east. Firstly, the *koine hodos,* the common highway, was a very important overland route which went from Ephesus up the Maeander Valley to Tralles, Nysa, Antiocheia and onwards to the river Euphrates and beyond. Secondly, from Ephesus one could travel to Sardis and then on the ancient Persian Royal Road which went to Susa; this became the primary means of linking Ephesus with the province of Galatia. Thus the two great trade-routes from the Euphrates both ended at Ephesus."[104]

---

[104] Gill, *op. cit.,* 308

Ephesus was also blessed by other circumstances that generated a lot of traffic through the city and with that traffic, great wealth. All of Rome's governmental communications with Asia and beyond went through its headquarters in Ephesus. The central tax collection office for all of Asia was in Ephesus as well. And, perhaps most importantly, Ephesus was home to the legal system for the region. All the major trials were held in Ephesus. Dio Chrysostom, a Greek orator who was a contemporary of Paul, described the impact of holding major trials in a city:

> 'The courts ... bring together an unnumbered throng of people—litigants, jurymen, orators, princes, attendants, slaves, pimps, muleteers, hucksters, harlots, and artisans. Consequently not only can those who have goods to sell obtain the highest prices, but also nothing in the city is out of work, neither the teams nor the houses nor the women. And this contributes not a little to prosperity; for where the greatest throng of people comes together, there necessarily we find money in greatest abundance, and it stands to reason that the place should thrive. ... So it is, you see, that the business of the courts is deemed of highest importance toward a city's strength and all men are interested in that as in nothing else.[105]

---

[105] Gill *op. cit.*, 309-310

It is not difficult, then to see why Paul wanted to go to Ephesus from the very beginning. Anything preached in Ephesus had a good chance of being spread all around the province of Asia just because of the exposure to so many people. What did the city look like when Paul got there? Many of the most impressive buildings tourists see today were not yet there when Paul walked into Ephesus. Among these are the famous Library of Celsus (125 AD) which today dominates the main street of Ephesus, The Temple of Hadrian (135 AD), and the Odeion (150 A.D)—the little theatre.

But the main street was there, lined by a colonnaded walkway as in all Greek cities, and there was the usual collection of sites: the Agora where business was conducted ringed by public buildings, various temples and the Great Theatre. In Acts 19:29 those who were enraged about Christian preaching rushed into that theatre. The theatre in Ep hesus was built into the western slope of Mt. Pion, and was wider than a football field. The seating capacity was perhaps about 20,000. The theater was some three hundred years old when Paul was in Ephesus.

"In the Graeco-Roman period, the theatre was one of a city's most important and impressive institutions. Activities other than the production of plays occurred in the theatre. The theatre in Ephesus was the regular meeting place of the assembly. A theatre could also be the site for mass meetings and official civic gatherings, such as the reading of imperial edicts. Further, prayers and sacrifice on behalf of the welfare of the city and civic festivals were a conducted in the theatre."[106]

Unfortunately, there are no remains today of the most significant building in Ephesus in Paul's time. That building was the famous Temple of Artemis. It was considered one of the seven wonders of the world[107] by many. It was four times as large as the Parthenon in Athens! One ancient writer recorded his impression of the temple this way:

> "I have set eyes on the wall of lofty Babylon on which is a road for chariots, and the statue of Zeus by the Alpheus, and the hanging gardens, and the colossus of the Sun, and the huge labour of the high pyramids, and the vast tomb of Mausolus; but when I saw the house of Artemis that mounted to the clouds, those other marvels lost their brilliancy,

[106] Gill, *op. cit.*, 348-349

[107] "I have seen the walls and Hanging Gardens of ancient Babylon, the statue of Olympian Zeus, the Colossus of Rhodes, the mighty work of the high Pyramids and the tomb of Mausolus. But when I saw the temple at Ephesus rising to the clouds, all these other wonders were put in the shade"- Philon of Byzantium cited from: http://www.unmuseum.org/ephesus.htm.

and I said, 'Lo, apart from Olympus, the Sun never looked on aught so grand."[108]

This building and the culture that surrounded it forms the background for the most dramatic episode in Paul's experience at Ephesus so it warrants a closer examination than the other buildings.

The Temple of Artemis

The Greek goddess Artemis was worshipped in many cities around the Mediterranean world but the Artemis worshipped in Ephesus was the most widely known and most distinctive version of this deity. "It was the cult of the Ephesian Artemis which, more than anything else, made Ephesus a centre of religious life during our period. But the influence of the cult of Artemis extended beyond the religious sphere to the civic, economic, and cultural life of the city."[109] Artemis was looked upon by the people of Ephesus as the one who answered their prayers, gave them direction for life and kept them safe and prosperous. She was revered much as Jesus is revered by Christians today! Her worship had been a significant part of the life of Ephesus for eight hundred years. The city of Ephesus saw itself as the defender of the worship of Artemis and also as its greatest missionary proponent. The great temple was destroyed and rebuilt many times. The temple that was

---

[108] Antipater, *Greek Anthology* (IX.58)

[109] Gill, *op. cit.*, 316

154

there when Paul got to Ephesus was re-built in the 4th century B.C. after a fire destroyed the earlier temple.

The temple was actually more than a mile outside the city of Ephesus. The original temple was built in a marshy area but after each destruction and re-building the temple was elevated. The final temple stood on a platform some thirteen steps above the ground. There were two rows of eight granite columns across the front and three rows of twenty-one columns down the sides. The columns were sixty feet high. Inside the temple stood the magnificent image of Artemis herself. The original image is no longer in existence but smaller copies of her show what she would have looked like. She is surrounded with imagery. Around her head is a wreath of wheat. Around her skirt are animals indicating her relationship to hunting. The many protrusions from the mid-section of her statue may be breasts but most scholars think not. Whatever these appendages depict they seem to represent Artemis as the source of fertility and sustenance.

In order to understand the furor that erupted over Paul's preaching in Ephesus, we need to know not only what the temple looked like but something of its relationship to the city. We have already said that there were temples dedicated to the worship of Artemis of Ephesus all over Asia and beyond that considered Ephesus the "mother church" of them all. Thus any threat to the reputation of the temple of Artemis in Ephesus would also repre-sent a threat to the status of the city in the whole Roman Province.

This in turn would affect the number of visitors and worshippers who came to Ephesus. In addition to the economic role that the temple played because of its religious influence in the region, the temple had become something like a little Switzerland to the Roman world. The temple of Artemis was considered so sacred that it was thought to be absolutely safe as a place to deposit money and other treasures both by individuals and by cities. A contemporary of Paul whom we have mentioned before, Dio Chrysostom, described the banking aspects of the temple of Artemis like this:

> You know about the Ephesians, of course, and that large sums of money are in their hands, some of it belonging to private citizens and deposited in the temple of Artemis, not alone money of the Ephesians but also of aliens and of persons from all parts of the world, and in some cases of commonwealths and kings, money which all deposit there in order that it may be safe, since no one has ever dared to violate that place, although countless wars have occurred in the past and the city has often been captured.[110]

Because of all the money in its vaults, the temple could loan money and make purchases of large tracts of land making it the largest land owner in the region and at the same time enhancing the reputation of the city of Ephesus in the region.

Thus the preaching of Paul touched not only the soul of the city but its wallet as well.

---

[110] Gill, *op. cit.*, 324-325.

Paul's Experience in Ephesus

As is usually the case, Luke has provided glimpses of what went on in Ephesus but there are many things we wish he had shared with us. For one thing, Luke has not said anything about Paul writing any of his letters from Ephesus, and it is clear that some, if not most, of his letters were written while he was there. It is very difficult to be certain where Paul's letters originated but his letters to Corinth and Philemon were certainly penned while he was ministering in Ephesus. Colossians also seems to have come from Ephesus (which is not far from Colossae) but many scholars think it does not sound like Paul. Romans may have been written just after he left Ephesus but surely a work like that would take some time—time when he wasn't walking!—and I wonder if he did not work on it in Ephesus. Of course the letter to Ephesus itself probably was written from Rome. All in all, however, we can conclude that while Paul was working full time to support himself and his ministry[111] and experiencing extreme emotional distress[112] and preaching Christ so effectively that he got the attention of the leadership of the economic segments of the city of Ephesus, he was also ministering to Christians in Macedonia, Greece and the interior of Asia by the written word. Think what he would have done if he'd had the internet!

---

[111] Acts 20:34-"You yourselves know that these hands ministered to my necessities, and to those who were with me."

[112] 2 Corinthians 1:8-"For we do not want you to be ignorant, brethren, of the affliction we experienced in Asia; for we were so utterly, unbearably crushed that we despaired of life itself. Why, we felt that we had received the sentence of death ..."

Luke also neglects to tell us what caused Paul's despair in Ephesus. When Paul wrote to the Corinthians, he mentioned that he was "unbearably crushed"[113] while he was in Asia.[114] Some scholars think that Paul was actually imprisoned while in Ephesus. They point to Paul's remarks to the Corinthians that "I die every day! What do I gain if, humanly speaking, I fought with beasts at Ephesus?"[115] When we read Luke's account of Paul's time in Ephesus there is nothing to suggest that Paul faced such terrible danger. Even in the account of Paul's conflict with Demetrius and the silversmiths Luke does not say that Paul was personally dragged into the theatre by the mob as were some of his colleagues.

But Luke does tell us of the impact that Paul's preaching had on the city of Ephesus and that was significant. When Paul arrived in Ephesus, he says he found twelve disciples. Since these twelve were part of the synagogue they were either Jews or Gentiles who had accepted the basic principles of Judaism. These "disciples" had also accepted Jesus as Messiah but had not been baptized in Jesus' name. Luke tells us that Paul spent three months presenting his case in the synagogue and when some in the synagogue began "speaking evil of the Way" Paul withdrew and the twelve disciples followed.

---

[113] See above, 2 Corinthians 1:8.

[114] Unless his pain has something to do with the fact that he was forbidden to preach in Asia on his first trip across Asia Minor which Luke does record. We don't know how much conflict and with whom this setback involved.

[115] I Corinthians 15:32

him. Paul moved to "the hall of Tyrannus" and we can only assume that Tyrannus was either one of the disciples or someone who was sympathetic with Paul's message. Paul spent two years teaching and preaching from his base in the Hall of Tyrannus and was so successful that some "itinerant Jewish exorcists" tried to copy him but failed publically.

After Paul had decided to leave Ephesus and return to Jerusalem, a leading businessman in the city, Demetrius the Silversmith, organized the craftsmen of the city to oppose Paul's message. The information we looked at earlier tells us why he was so upset. Paul's message of a living God who created the world and could not be represented by a man-made object struck at the very heart of the worship of Artemis, a worship that had a history of more than five hundred years in the city and by which Ephesus was known throughout the world. If Paul's message won a significant number of converts the image of Artemis would suffer and there would be fewer tourists and there would be less market for the goods produced by the craftsmen. Of all the mobs Paul ever faced, apparently this one was the worst. It was finally quelled only when the city official in charge of the government warned the people that they "were in danger of being charged with rioting today, there being no cause that we can give to justify this commotion."[116] A charge of rioting would get the attention of Rome and there would be consequences. Luke always went out of his way to show that Rome did not find fault with Christians. The town clerk declared that "these men here who are neither sacrilegious nor blasphemers of our goddess" were being treated illegally—they were innocent. Luke had already noted that

---

[116] Acts 18:40

"most of them [in the mob] did not know why they had come together."

Conclusion

Once again, Luke has shown us the Gospel let loose in the Roman world. Luke begins his account of Paul's missionary activity by telling us that Paul was hindered from preaching the Gospel in Asia. He then describes time and again how Paul managed to survive the beatings, imprisonments, hardships, poverty, and hatred this message evoked. Not only did he survive, he succeeded. There may only have been one or two or twelve Christians in a city but every city except Athens had a church and was part of the body of Christ. It is entirely fitting that Luke ends his second book with Paul confined in jail but the Gospel let loose in the capital of the Roman Empire.

Chapter 12

Rome: The City That Let Loose Paul's Gospel

It may be doubted that Rome should be included in a book on *St. Paul and the Cities*. There is no evidence that Paul ever saw the Coliseum or any of the other major buildings in Rome. He entered the city as a prisoner guarded by a soldier named Julius and was promptly handed over to the Roman authorities. Luke records in the book of Acts that Paul was allowed to stay in quarters that he rented for two whole years (Acts 28:30), but if he was allowed to leave these quarters and go abroad in the city attached to a soldier we have no account of it. Luke tells us that he welcomed "all who came to him," but he gives us no clue as to how many came or who they were. Apparently Paul never had the opportunity to visit a synagogue much less speak to a congregation about how Christ's death on a cross fulfilled the prophecies found in the Hebrew Bible. Paul saw Rome from the limited perspective of his apartment; he did not have the opportunity to speak to crowds and present his Gospel to them.

On the other hand, Rome was the opposite of Las Vegas and nothing that happened there stayed there! Luke tells us that Paul "welcomed all who came to him, preaching the kingdom of God and teaching about the Lord Jesus Christ quite openly and unhindered." The sentence does not seem strange to Christians who come across it in their daily Bible readings, but to scholars who read it in the original Greek it seems like an unfinished sentence. Either Luke was not able to finish his sentence or he left it that way on purpose. One Baptist scholar[117] writing in the middle of the last century argued persuasively that Luke intended the sentence to stand exactly as it is to express the truth that though Paul was shut up in his room and facing death, the Gospel he preached had been let loose in the world and there was no period at the end of its sentence. The good news was unhindered and set free to go through the Roman empire and beyond.

Rome In Paul's Day

Paul would have entered Rome through one of its sixteen gates, probably the one known as the Porta Capena. This was the gate through which the Appian Way entered the city. Travellers who arrived in Italy by boat, as Paul and his group did, would have walked from Puteoli on the Bay of Naples to Capua to reach the Appian Way. When Paul arrived at the city gate, Rome was home to about a million people, a size it maintained for the next century before declining. In physical size it was the largest city in the empire. Paul's route from the Porta Capena to the Praetorian Barracks would have taken him diagonally northeast all the way across the city, a distance of at least three to four miles. It is quite possible that this first walk across the city was also Paul's last exposure to the great buildings in the heart of

---

[117] Frank Stagg, *The Book of Acts: The Early Struggle for an Unhindered Gospel* (Nashville, Broadman Press 1955).

Rome. Upon reaching the headquarters of the Praetorian Guard, the centurion who had accompanied Paul all the way from Caesarea and survived a shipwreck with him would have officially handed him over to his superiors. We know that two days later Paul was settled in rented quarters where he could receive company, but Luke does not tell us Paul's initial circumstances. Was he placed in a cell? How did he find a place to rent? Presumably both Luke and Aristarchus who accompanied Paul on this last voyage were free to handle the search for a room and find food for Paul. Julius, the Centurion, would have delivered to his superiors whatever documents he had brought with him concerning Paul unless these had been destroyed in the wreck of their ship. And then began what turned out to be at least a two year wait for Paul's fate to be decided.

At the point where Luke's narrative in the book of Acts ends, Paul is still under house arrest and chained to a soldier. It is unclear whether Paul was released from this imprisonment and continued his ministry for two or three more years. The Pastoral Epistles (1 and 2 Timothy and Titus) seem to have been written after the book of Acts ends, but many scholars consider these works to have been written by Paul's disciples in his name because these letters seem to reflect a period after Paul's time. Early Christian tradition states that both Peter and Paul were executed by Nero sometime between 64 and 68 AD. A sudden execution of Paul may well have forced Luke to cease his writing, but it is also possible that Luke stopped his narrative with the expectation of writing a third volume about the expansion of the Christian faith north and east of the areas Paul evangelized.

The Jews in Rome

For centuries, beginning at least in the sixth century BC when the Babylonians conquered Israel and took many into captivity, Jews began to leave Israel and migrate in every direction. It is evident from Luke's narrative in the book of Acts that there were synagogues and established Jewish communities in most if not all the cities Paul touched. Jews who lived outside Israel were said to be part of the Diaspora, a Greek term that means "the dispersion." Paul himself, a native of Tarsus in Cilicia (now Turkey), was a part of the Diaspora. It is not surprising that Rome attracted all kinds of people because of its power and size. Apparently many Jews had made their way to Rome by the time of Paul because it is estimated that Jews composed some ten percent of the entire population which would mean that there were about forty-five thousand Jews in Rome.[118] While this estimate may well be high, there is no doubt that there were many Jews and many synagogues in the city. Judaism was recognized as a legal religion from the time of Caesar Augustus on--another indication that the Jewish community was a large one.

It appears that one of the very first things Paul did upon arriving in Rome was to contact the Jewish community leaders.

---

[118] Rodney Stark, *The Triumph of Christianity: How the Jesus Movement Became the World's Largest Religion.* (HarperCollins. Kindle Edition.,2011) 163, Location 2648.

Luke does not give us any indication of how many Jewish leaders Paul reached out to, but the group that came to talk to him could obviously fit in the apartment which Paul had rented. That first meeting resulted in a second meeting with a larger group but the group still met in Paul's apartment. Here is the way the book of Acts describes that first meeting with Jewish leaders in Rome:

> When they had appointed a day for him, they came to him at his lodging in great numbers. And he expounded the matter to them from morning till evening, testifying to the kingdom of God and trying to convince them about Jesus both from the law of Moses and from the prophets. And some were convinced by what he said, while others disbelieved. So, as they disagreed among themselves, they departed, after Paul had made one statement: "The Holy Spirit was right in saying to your fathers through Isaiah the prophet:
>
> 'Go to this people, and say,
> You shall indeed hear but never understand,
> and you shall indeed see but never perceive.
> For this people's heart has grown dull,
> and their ears are heavy of hearing,
> and their eyes they have closed;

lest they should perceive with their eyes,

and hear with their ears,

and understand with their heart,

and turn for me to heal them.'

Let it be known to you then that this salvation of
God has been sent to the Gentiles; they will listen."[119]

It would appear that while some may have been convinced by
Paul's argument, the majority were not. Since Luke's narrative
ends at this point we have no record of follow-up meetings between Paul and such groups except for the note that Paul "lived
there two whole years at his own expense, and welcomed all who
came to him, preaching the kingdom of God and teaching about
the Lord Jesus Christ quite openly and unhindered."[120]

It is interesting that the Jewish leaders who came to hear
Paul that day had heard nothing about him. Luke notes that they
said:

"We have received no letters from Judea about
you, and none of the brethren coming here has reported or spoken any evil about you. [22] But we desire to hear from you what your views are; for with

[119] Acts 28:17-28

[120] Acts 29:30-31

regard to this sect we know that everywhere it is spoken against."[121]

Whether the Jewish leadership in Jerusalem had not followed up to make their case against Paul by sending information about him other than what the centurion, Julius, carried on his person or whether they tried to do so but were delayed by a shipwreck or other travel difficulties we do not know. Since Paul's group was delayed several months any delegates sent from Jerusalem should have arrived in Rome before them but no such delegation had contacted the Jewish community in Rome.

The Christians in Rome

There were Christians in Rome before Paul got there. At least five years before Paul arrived at Puteoli to begin his walk to Rome he had written a letter to Roman Christians--the now famous *Romans* in the Bible. Before that, Paul had come in contact with two Christians, Aquila and Priscilla who had just left Rome after the Emperor Claudius expelled all Jews from Rome in 49 AD.[122] Claudius expelled Jews from Rome because there had been a conflict within the Jewish community over one "Chrestus" which must have spilled over into the larger community. [123]

---

[121] Acts 28:21-22

[122] Acts 18:2

[123] "Since the Jews constantly made disturbances at the instigation of Chrestus, he [the Emperor Claudius] expelled them from Rome." Suetonius, *The*

The "Chrestus" looks a lot like "Christ" and it is assumed that the root of the disturbance was a conflict between Jews who had become Christians and those who had not. How long had there been Christians before their presence became obvious in the Roman community? No one knows for sure, but it is clear that Christians made their way to cities that had seaports very early, and Rome was the destination of most of the grain ships that passed by the Eastern Mediterranean home of the faith. So within twenty years of Jesus' crucifixion and possibly much earlier than that Christians had taken the faith to Rome.

Luke tells us that Paul intended to go to Rome[124] after he took the offering he had collected to Jerusalem. In his letter to the Romans Paul wrote that he wished to take the Gospel to Spain and visit Rome on his way there:

> I have longed for many years to come to you, I hope to see you in passing as I go to Spain, and to be sped on my journey there by you, once I have enjoyed your company for a little. At present, however, I am going to Jerusalem with aid for the saints. [125]

Lives of the Twelve Caesars by Gaius Suetonius Tranquillus, translated by J. C. Rolfe, 25. Accessed from https://en.wikisource.org/wiki/The_Lives_of_the_ Twelve_ Caesars/Claudius#25.

[124] Acts 19:21

[125] Romans 15:24-25

Upon arriving in Italy after spending a winter on Malta, Luke notes that Paul and his group "found brethren, and were invited to stay with them for seven days." How he "found brethren" Luke does not tell us. While these "brethren" could be Jews Luke seems to mean that these were Christian "brethren." Apparently the Christians were well known enough for Paul to find them by asking people at the dock! Whether this was one man and his family with whom Paul and his group stayed or a community of Christians, Luke does not say. Normally when Paul entered a new city his first stop was the synagogue but apparently that is not the case here.

The next Christians Paul encountered were from Rome itself but Paul met them 43 miles south of Rome at a place called the Forum (Market) of Appius which must have been the ancient equivalent of a rest stop on an Interstate highway or the first exit after a long stretch without much service. It was well known as a stopping place. Here is the way Luke describes the encounter.

> And the brethren there, when they heard of us, came as far as the Forum of Ap'pius and Three Taverns to meet us. On seeing them Paul thanked God and took courage. [126]

Luke does not tell us how news of Paul's arrival in Italy had reached Rome before them. Did the Christians in Puteoli send

---

[126] Acts 28:15

word to Christians in Rome about Paul? They must have, but the 170 miles to Rome would not have been a trivial trip. Why did someone make that trip? How did Christians in Puteoli know how to contact Christians in Rome? Obviously, Luke has left us with more questions than answers.

How many Christians were there in Rome when Paul arrived there. Exact numbers are not possible to come by, but scholars have been able to project backward from known population levels to come up with ballpark figures. One recent scholar has concluded there were seven hundred Christians in Rome in the year 100.[127] It would be reasonable to assume that there were less than 100 there when Paul arrived in the early 60's--perhaps 50-60 Christians. Such a number would indicate that ten to fifteen families made up the Roman congregations. Since no church buildings were involved yet, this means that small groups of Christians met in homes. While this projection may seem very small, it is in line with the evidence we do have. For example, the sixteenth chapter of Romans lists numbers of people presumably in Rome to whom Paul sends greetings along with his long letter. Paul names twenty-six individuals plus the members of several families. He says that several of these people have worked with him in the past or spent time in prison with him. He notes that two of these Roman Christians, Andronicus and Junias, were "in Christ" before he was--that is they had been

---

[127] Stark, *ibid.*

Christians longer than Paul himself. Indeed, if another scholar[128] is correct, Junias is none other than the wife of Chuza mentioned in Luke 8:3 as being one of three women who provided for Jesus from their means. Paul says that they were "in Christ" before him and since he became a Christian within two or three years of Jesus' crucifixion, Chuza and Joanna (Andronicus and Junia) must have been among the original disciples who were part of the Jerusalem church. So Paul may have known personally a sizeable percentage of all the Christians in Rome.

The fact that Paul seems to have known so many of the Roman Christians even though he had never been to Rome makes Luke's description of his stay in Rome somewhat puzzling. Luke describes two meetings with Jewish leaders and says Paul welcomed all who came to him, preaching and teaching "about the Lord Jesus Christ quite openly and unhindered."[129] But there is not a word about any of the twenty-six people to whom he sent greetings coming to see him! It seems highly un-

---

[128] Bauckham, R. (2002). *Gospel Women: Studies of the Named Women in the Gospels* (p. 184). Grand Rapids, MI; Cambridge, U.K.: William B. Eerdmans Publishing Company. "The similarity in sound of Junia to the Hebrew name Joanna (Yehohannah or Yohannah) is quite close, as close as many of the known equivalences listed above [such as Paul/Saul]. This opens the way to the suggestion that the Junia of Romans 16:7 is the same person as Luke's Joanna. That both were founding members of the Jerusalem church gives this suggestion considerable plausibility. It has always seemed remarkable that Paul could call two apostles of whom we never hear anywhere else in early Christian literature "prominent among the apostles" (Rom 16:7). Perhaps we do in fact hear of at least one of these in Luke's Gospel, where she is already prominent among the women followers of Jesus."
[129] Acts 28:17-31.

likely that members of the Roman churches would walk forty-three miles to meet him at the Forum of Appius yet not come see him in the city! Perhaps the reason Luke does not describe such scenes is that he was hastening to the end of his book or, perhaps, he did not see a need to mention Paul's interaction with the Christian community. We wish he could have continued.

Not only did Luke not tell us who visited Paul, neither did he mention the letter to the Romans. The absence of any reference to the letter is not unusual for Luke. Luke did not mention Paul's ministry of letter writing at all in the book of Acts. He could have cut short many scholarly debates had he just mentioned that Paul wrote a letter from some of the cities in which he worked. It is hard not to be curious about the reception Paul's letter to the church in Rome got. Were they awed by its erudition? Did they debate Paul's reasoning? Did they have other letters of Paul with which to place Romans? Was one person given the responsibility for keeping the letter? Did they treat Paul's letter as scripture as soon as it was received or only later? Did they make copies of the letter and send it to other congregations such as the one at Puteoli? Unfortunately answers to most of these questions are impossible to come by.

Paul's Ministry to Rome

Given that Paul had very little opportunity to move about the city of Rome one might assume that Paul did not have a ministry to Rome. Such an assumption would, however, be very questionable. Paul himself apparently thought his ministry there, limited as it was, had profound results in at least two areas. To see what he thought he accomplished we need to read his letter to the Philippian church. While it is not absolutely certain that Paul was imprisoned in Rome when he wrote this letter, it seems likely that that was the case. If so, then what he says there gives us information about how he saw the impact of his time in Rome. Here is what he wrote:

> I want you to know, brethren, that what has happened to me has really served to advance the gospel, so that it has become known throughout the whole praetorian guard and to all the rest that my imprisonment is for Christ; and most of the brethren have been made confident in the Lord because of my imprisonment, and are much more bold to speak the word of God without fear.[130]

Paul asserted that his imprisonment had an effect both within the ranks of the military who were assigned to guard him and within the Christian community. Luke does not tell us much about the physical arrangements involved in keeping Paul under house arrest. Paul mentions that he was in chains so apparently he was connected to a soldier with a short chain, but was he chained to a soldier at night as he slept as well as through the day? Luke does not tell us, but we must assume that at least during the day Paul had a captive audience just as the centurion had

---

[130] Philippians 1:12-14

a captive prisoner. As Paul taught day by day scores of soldiers had no choice but to listen to him. When he prayed or sang the soldier listened. As he argued with the leadership of the Jewish community, the soldier heard the dialogue. In time, all the soldiers knew about this prisoner who testified daily about Christ. Doubtless some were convinced that Paul was right, and, thus it was that awareness of the gospel message spread throughout the ranks of the elite soldiers who were kept in Rome at the heart of the Empire. Paul wrote that in addition to "the whole praetorian guard" he also had been able to advance the gospel to "all the rest." He does not tell us whom "the rest" included it might be possible that the soldiers to whom Paul talked during the day repeated what they heard outside the barracks as well. Thus Paul's ministry in Rome may well have had more impact than his work in other cities.

In addition to making soldiers aware of his mission, Paul says his prison ministry had an effect on Christians who were not captives. Because faith in Christ had become a normal part of each day's conversation even among Roman soldiers, ordinary Christians also felt comfortable giving their own testimonies. Paul goes on to mention that there may have been some who preached Christ for the wrong reasons.

> Some indeed preach Christ from envy and rivalry,
> but others from good will. The latter do it out of
> love, knowing that I am put here for the defense

of the gospel; the former proclaim Christ out of partisanship, not sincerely but thinking to afflict me in my imprisonment. What then? Only that in every way, whether in pretense or in truth, Christ is proclaimed; and in that I rejoice.[131]

The exact nature of the envy and rivalry Paul cites is not clear, but it is clear that Paul's imprisonment caused some controversy in the Christian community. Perhaps the obvious impact Paul's witnessing was having caused some who were less impressive preachers and teachers to be jealous. Perhaps they found something about Paul's preaching they opposed and then spent a lot of time preaching their version of the gospel. Either way, Paul counted the increased preaching as part of his legacy in Rome!

Conclusion

Catholics have long contended that Peter played a primary role in the church at Rome. While that may be the case, it is clear that Paul's role, even under such adverse circumstances, was significant. Rome was destined to become the leading church in the Roman Empire and play a major role in shaping the thinking of Christians for a thousand years. Both Paul and Peter were executed by the emperor Nero sometime in the mid-sixties but their legacy lives on to this day.

It is fitting that we end a book about "St. Paul and the Cities" in Rome. Paul had intended just to make a passing visit

---

[131] Philippians 1:15-18

to the city on his way to mission fields where none had worked. He never intended to make this great city part of his legacy, but the letter he wrote them and the message he delivered from their jail have dominated Christian theology to this day. Gentiles the world over owe the last apostle a great debt.

Made in the USA
Columbia, SC
22 October 2017